101 WAYS TO USE SOCIAL MEDIA TO DO GOOD

FRANCES LEARY

BALBOA
PRESS
A DIVISION OF HAY HOUSE

Copyright © 2018 Frances Leary.

All rights reserved. No part of this book may be used or reproduced by any means, graphic, electronic, or mechanical, including photocopying, recording, taping or by any information storage retrieval system without the written permission of the author except in the case of brief quotations embodied in critical articles and reviews.

Balboa Press books may be ordered through booksellers or by contacting:

Balboa Press
A Division of Hay House
1663 Liberty Drive
Bloomington, IN 47403
www.balboapress.com
1 (877) 407-4847

Because of the dynamic nature of the Internet, any web addresses or links contained in this book may have changed since publication and may no longer be valid. The views expressed in this work are solely those of the author and do not necessarily reflect the views of the publisher, and the publisher hereby disclaims any responsibility for them.

The author of this book does not dispense medical advice or prescribe the use of any technique as a form of treatment for physical, emotional, or medical problems without the advice of a physician, either directly or indirectly. The intent of the author is only to offer information of a general nature to help you in your quest for emotional and spiritual well-being. In the event you use any of the information in this book for yourself, which is your constitutional right, the author and the publisher assume no responsibility for your actions.

Any people depicted in stock imagery provided by Getty Images are models, and such images are being used for illustrative purposes only. Certain stock imagery © Getty Images.

This book is a work of non-fiction. Unless otherwise noted, the author and the publisher make no explicit guarantees as to the accuracy of the information contained in this book and in some cases, names of people and places have been altered to protect their privacy.

Print information available on the last page.

ISBN: 978-1-9822-0321-4 (sc)
ISBN: 978-1-9822-0320-7 (hc)
ISBN: 978-1-9822-0322-1 (e)

Library of Congress Control Number: 2018905148

Balboa Press rev. date: 05/15/2018

For Brynn
and
the Future Generation of *Soul*cializers

ACKNOWLEDGMENTS

First and foremost, I want to thank social media users worldwide, especially those of you with whom I am directly connected. Without you this book would never have come to be.

I am eternally grateful to Dr. Joe Vitale, Mike Dooley, and Lisa Arie for their early endorsements of this work. Thank you for believing in the transformative nature of this book and for seeing its potential.

Special thanks to Susan Cooper and Laurie Dolhan for your wisdom as readers. Your editorial recommendations have challenged me and kept me accountable to producing work that is completely in alignment with who I am.

Thank you also to Mary Jane Copps for a writing day spent together several years ago when I saw the first parts of this book really come into fruition.

Thank you to Amy McNaughton, whose ongoing support has helped me stay true to myself and what I am creating in my life.

Thank you to everyone who responded to my online requests for inspiring content, including: Augustine, Nick, Lorelei, Joy, Jennifer, Natalie, Kathy, Judith, Stephanie, Rakale, Rachel, Turner, Marietta, Karen, Mary Jo, Tracy, Elisa, Carolyn, Angie, Matt, Whitney, Billie, Audrey, Cathy, and Rosie.

Thank you to the editorial and design team at Balboa Press for lending your expert skills to this project.

Special thanks to Richard and Susan Cooper, for fostering my beliefs in the goodness of people and the beauty of life since birth, and to Anne Cooper for always believing in me.

I want to thank my daughter Brynn, whose magical outlook

on life gives me daily hope that what's written in this book will be embraced by the upcoming generation of social media users.

I want to thank my husband, Del, for loving me as I am, supporting my pursuits of happiness, and sharing in this daily adventure of life.

Finally, I want to thank all of you who are with me on this journey to use social media for good.

CONTENTS

Preface xiii
Introduction xvii

1.	Show Up and Be Yourself	1
2.	Think Before You Post	3
3.	Like It	5
4.	Use Reactions	7
5.	Step Off the Lectern	8
6.	Step Away	10
7.	Be Safe on Social Media	12
8.	Engage with The Universe	14
9.	Celebrate Birthdays	16
10.	Give Quick Warnings	18
11.	Sign on the (Virtual) Dotted Line	19
12.	Keep Relationship Updates Offline	21
13.	Don't Just Tell…Show	22
14.	Avoid Fake News	23
15.	Remember Your Children Will Grow Up ...	26
16.	Be Upworthy	28
17.	Friend Authentically	29
18.	Smile while You Post	31
19.	Answer Questions	32
20.	Share What Is Meaningful	33
21.	Comment and Reply	34
22.	Be Constructive in Sharing Dislikes	35
23.	Avoid the Fake Perfect Phenomenon	36
24.	Learn	38

25.	Mention and Tag	39
26.	Click a Link	41
27.	Use Emojis	42
28.	Beware Sharing Too Many Selfies	43
29.	TEDify Your Social Media	44
30.	Like a Page	45
31.	Support a Cause	46
32.	Craftify Your Kid-dom	48
33.	Share Content from Not-for-Profit Organizations	49
34.	Support Businesses You Believe In	51
35.	Share Your Tips	52
36.	Don't Spam via Your Messages on LinkedIn	53
37.	Unite	55
38.	Really Mean It	56
39.	Like and Follow Your Favorite Not-for-Profit Organizations	57
40.	Stay in Touch with Current Events	58
41.	Celebrate Success	59
42.	Make Yourself Available to Others	61
43.	Don't Post in Anger	63
44.	Leave Your Crankiness Offline	65
45.	Make Someone's Day	66
46.	Research	68
47.	Share Inspiring Quotes	70
48.	Personalize LinkedIn Messages	72
49.	Share What Makes You Laugh	74
50.	Engage on Community Bulletin Boards	75
51.	Don't Be a Bystander	76
52.	Understand Your Motivations	78
53.	Avoid Replacing Friends with Page Likes	79
54.	Define Your Personal Boundaries	81
55.	Share What Makes You Happy	83
56.	Say Thank You	85
57.	Recommend Your Favorite Things	87

58. Avoid Posting What Could Hurt Someone Else 88
59. Share Inspiring Images 89
60. Play 91
61. Look Up 92
62. Watch Your Language 93
63. Work Virtually 95
64. Avoid PUI (Posting Under the Influence) 96
65. Have a Family Social Media Contract 98
66. Lend Support through Kiva 100
67. Know When Not to Like or Follow a Business 101
68. Only Like a Post or Tweet if You Really Like It 102
69. Pay It Forward 103
70. Take Care When Engaging in Online Debate 104
71. Don't Share Photos of Others They Wouldn't Post Themselves 106
72. Give a KICKStart 108
73. Send Personal Messages 109
74. Share Helpful Information 110
75. Boost Your PLN 111
76. Share a Favorite Recipe 112
77. Serve Up Some Soul Food 114
78. Cull Responsibly and Respectfully 115
79. Be a Dodo 117
80. Understand the Lack of Tone 118
81. Share Videos You Love 119
82. Invite People to Groups 121
83. Join the Cheer Squad 123
84. Filter Your Filters 124
85. Bridge the Generation Gap 126
86. Get Face to Face 128
87. Know Where Your Kids Spend Time 129
88. Avoid Anything Too Personal 130
89. Seek Help 131
90. Stay Open-Minded 132

91.	Give Help	134
92.	Promote Events	135
93.	Celebrate Your Own Success	136
94.	Respond	137
95.	Recommend Favorite Places	138
96.	Use Share Buttons	140
97.	Avoid Using Share Buttons	141
98.	Tell Your Story	142
99.	Raise Your Voice	145
100.	Observe Moments of Silence	146
101.	Be Soulcial	147
	References	155

PREFACE

Full disclosure: I'm one of *those* people. You know, one of those positive glass-is-half-full kind of people. I wear my rose-colored glasses with pride on a daily basis, knowing, without doubt, that my choice to see good in life consistently creates more of it.

This philosophy of living wasn't a choice I made at any one point in my life. It's a choice I make every day. From the time I was a little girl, I've believed that people are innately good. No matter what is happening around us, if we look closely enough, we can find some element of goodness in every circumstance. I also believe that our thoughts, words, and actions work collectively to create the world in which we live. So, I look closely, I find the good in life, and I consciously choose thoughts, words, and actions that will make the world a better place.

My greatest hope is that my choices will inspire others, especially my daughter, to do the same, and I would have never predicted that social media would become a primary vehicle for me to inspire this change.

While it's hard for me to believe now, I was slow in adapting to the world of social media. I remember my husband on a vacation in Mexico checking out this newfangled whatchamacallit he referred to as *Facebook* and me thinking that I wasn't quite ready to embrace such a public forum as that.

Little did I know that social media would later become my lifeline in so many ways.

After moving from Texas to Newfoundland to Manitoba to Mississippi to Nova Scotia and finally to Colorado (whew, that's a lot of miles covered), I have friends scattered throughout North

America and some living on other continents around the globe. Social media has become my way of staying connected. Because of it, I have the privilege of seeing my friends' newborn babies, celebrating milestones with loved ones far away, and virtually participating in so many aspects of life that would otherwise go unknown. I have not yet abandoned, nor do I plan to abandon, the annual Christmas letter; however, that is one of the only times I send (or receive) physical mail throughout the year. Mailing those letters is a treasured experience, as is opening the ones I receive. In between those annual touchstones, social media creates an ongoing connection upon which friendships can build. I have come to treasure it for allowing me to stay so close to friends I value dearly across the miles.

My entrance into the world of social media came shortly after I had begun my entrepreneurial journey. As my marketing business grew, so did social media. In what seemed like no time, social media was no longer this newfangled whatchamacallit. It became one of the most powerful and transformational tools for my business and for all those I served.

Its transformation lies in the fact that social media is about people. It's about people connecting with people: meeting new people, building and strengthening relationships, and building bridges between humanity.

As I began to understand this transformative nature, I also began to note how social media can be used to cause harm. Although my rose-colored glasses hid this aspect of social media from me for some time, eventually it became clear as day. There are those who use social media to condemn, to tear down, to bully, to cheat, to lie, to hurt, to deceive…and the list goes on.

After making this discovery, I had to search myself to understand why, if my purpose is to focus on goodness and bring more goodness to the world, I was being bombarded with this negativity in my social feeds.

Then it became clear.

Knowing deep down that we are all beings of love and light, I came to recognize that most of the destruction on social media stems from the fact that many of us are not aware of the power of social media and the impact of how we use it.

This book was born out of my desire to shed light on that power and to raise our collective level of consciousness in communication.

Social media is a vehicle for us to express our thoughts, words, and actions, and as such, it is a vehicle through which we create the world in which we live.

If we, as social media users, know without a doubt that our words generate impact, and we also know that social media has a reach far beyond that which we can see, then we can begin to grasp this fact:

Every word we post online is a small ripple that makes a huge wave…a wave that cannot be stopped.

With every word we post, every like we click, we have a choice. By being mindful of our words and choosing to empower rather than to deflate, we become part of a global movement that is consciously choosing to make the world a better place, one social media post at a time. Together we can create a better world for our children.

I invite you to join me on that journey.

INTRODUCTION

Using social media to do good is something everyone can begin doing right now. It works on every social media platform. It works for personal use and for business. It is more of a philosophical approach to communication than a strategy, and it requires no specific age (other than that which is required by the platforms themselves) or gender or belief system. Everyone who engages on social media can use it for good.

This book identifies 101 very simple things that people can do, starting today. Some of the ideas mentioned may be more relatable by certain groups of people than by others, and other ideas are entirely universal. Before breaking down the ways one by one, I wanted to take the time to explore some overarching areas in our lives in which we can use social media for good.

Shifting Our Perspectives

Some of the most powerful ways we can use social media to do good focus entirely on our own internal beliefs and our approach to communication. We are taught from a very early age that our words have impact on others. We learn about the power of language to express love and support. We feel joy when we hear words that lift us up. We also feel the opposite impact when we experience words being used for manipulation or bullying or hate. We learn that sometimes different situations require different types of language and that some conversations are better if kept private. As we get older, we gain an understanding about how to choose our language based on situations. We may use different language in a work setting giving a tutorial to coworkers or at school giving a presentation than we would when chatting with friends over a campfire. The conversations we have and language we use in the bedroom most often stay there.

In each of these scenarios, whether at work or at home, in private or in public, we can show up fully, 100 percent authentically, and be ourselves. We simply choose which conversations to keep private, which can be public, and what type of language is appropriate for each situation. We also choose when to use no words at all, knowing that once we speak them we cannot take them back.

Somehow as social media has evolved, many of the lessons we have learned about how to engage in life have not entirely transferred to our use of social media.

We often don't keep those personal conversations private. We forget when to be quiet. We lose sight of the fact that engaging on social media is public, and sometimes we think we have to be someone other than who we are in order to be there.

None of this is true. To shift our use of social media in order to do good, we need to turn our attention inward and look at how we are showing up, what words we are using, and why we are there in the first place. Many of the ideas put forth in this book are aimed at supporting this personal journey.

Understanding the Power of Our Actions

Both offline and online, our actions have an impact. Every action we take results in something else. Although some of these results are microscopic and extremely difficult to see, they are still there, and their impacts grow over time.

Consider all the actions we can take when we engage on social media. We can like something, not like something, retweet something, comment on something, send messages, make connections, delete connections, join groups, post content, share reviews, and so much more.

Every action—*every* action—once done cannot be completely undone. Because of the nature of social media, once you take action, that action is out there for others to see. No matter how private you think your social media accounts are, no action taken on social media is private. You may delete something, but the impact of that initial action has already been felt by someone somewhere. No action on social media is small.

In order to do good on social media, we must understand how much power our actions truly have. Only then can we begin to consider what actions we want to take going forward.

Empowering Future Generations

Many children today seem to have been born with an iPad in their hands. Using technology to access online tools is second nature to them. Social media, however, is something that has to be taught. Sure, they can create an account and start posting pictures. They do not, however, know how to engage on social media responsibly. It is our responsibility (whether as parents, teachers, employers or other respected authority figures) to teach them.

Digital citizenship begins with knowledge and safety. From there it extends to many of the other concepts we are exploring in this book—how to use social media in a responsible way that will do good rather than harm to oneself or to others.

If we can empower our young people to have a solid understanding of social media and its power before or just as they become active engagers, we can empower an entire generation as ambassadors who use social media for good.

Sharing and Acquiring Knowledge

Knowledge sharing and acquisition are part of the very core nature of social media. When we post something on social media, we are sharing various forms of knowledge that are then acquired by others. This knowledge may be perceived or subjective knowledge in the form of one's own personal interpretations or belief systems. It can also be proven or objective knowledge in the form of facts, statistics, or figures. We are bombarded by a wide variety of knowledge every minute of every hour of every day (or at least every minute of every hour of every day that we choose to be online).

As both sharers and acquirers of knowledge, we have a choice. We choose what we share. We choose whether to perpetuate good will or judgment. We choose to fact-check or not. We choose to post in haste or to consider our words prior to sharing them with the world.

Similarly, we have a choice each time we see knowledge shared by others. We choose what action we take—whether to like it, share it, or hide it. We choose who we connect or do not connect with. We choose to take what is shared at face value or to do our own research to determine for ourselves what is true.

In order to use social media for good, we must be aware of the choices that we are making as we share and acquire knowledge, and we must make choices that will have positive impacts in our own lives and the lives of others.

Growing Professionally

Social media is a powerful tool for those who want to grow and expand their professional lives. It provides the opportunity for us to connect with individuals and organizations on a global scale.

This means that we have more access to resources from which we can learn. We also have easier access to universal tools we can use for communication, making networking and expanding our professional learning networks much easier. We can access tutorials, connect with mentors, conduct market research, and so much more.

However, there are some common practices that have evolved that are counterproductive. As professionals gain a more thorough understanding of how their actions on social media impact others, they can begin to shape their social media communication in a manner that generates a positive outcome for their own professional growth and in the lives of others.

Fueling Entrepreneurial and Business Growth

Social media is one of the most transformative tools for entrepreneurial and business growth. Businesses can use social media to reach their customers on a much larger scale than ever before. They can also use their social channels to extend their customer service and to create transformation through the work they do.

By using social media as an extension of the transformation provided through their products and services, businesses and entrepreneurs can serve their tribes in more powerful ways. Just consider how many lives can benefit from your gifts when you show up authentically and engage from a place of service.

In fact, I would suggest that not using social media might even limit the transformation that entrepreneurs could provide. When entrepreneurs and businesses focus their attention on engaging with the tribes they want to serve and using their social channels to help them provide solutions for them right now, lives are improved, and businesses are grown.

Consciously choosing to use social media for good as part of business development means being aware of the full impact of the online choices you make and then taking responsibility for those choices. The ideas shared in this book can support you in this journey.

Building Community

By engaging on social media, we become part of a community. Actually, we gain access to many communities. We can connect with local interest groups or support local organizations. We can also get connected to people around the world who share our same interests and values.

By understanding the resources that are available to us, we can choose to use social media to support the initiatives we believe in, whether they are close to home or on the other side of the world. We can learn to use social media to support organizations that are doing much-needed work on the ground in communities around the globe.

By understanding the impact of our words and our actions, we can begin to see that every post we make has the potential either to build community or tear it down.

Changing the World

It is through gaining insights into the transformative potential of social media in all these areas of our lives that we can create change. Every action we take on social media is a choice. Every action generates an impact.

Every social media user has the power to choose to take actions that do good and that generate a positive outcome in one's own life and in the lives of others.

Now magnify that by more than three billion social media users. Whew. That's a lot of positive action and a lot of positive impact.

By harnessing our collective use of social media to do good, together we can truly change the world.

1

SHOW UP AND BE YOURSELF

Social media is about relationships, and relationships are formed by real people connecting with each other. That's social media.

It isn't about numbers, such as how many friends, fans, or followers you have. It's not about how many times a day you post. It's not about making sales or converting friends to leads. It's simply about being where you are, meeting people where they are, being who you are, and connecting with others who are themselves.

It's also not about being perfect. You don't have to pretend to be the perfect parent or spouse. You don't have to pretend you have the perfect job or kids. We all know that's a sham. Nothing and no one is perfect. The only thing you're perfect at is being you, and that's who people want to connect with online.

There is no right way to be on social media other than to be yourself. Now, that doesn't mean you have to reveal every part of yourself at every moment of every day…but we'll save that for later.

If you have to be someone else, or if you're always there with an agenda, what's the point of being there at all?

People connect with you because you're you. So just be yourself. It really is that simple.

Action: Take a look at your social media channels. Look at your profiles, posts, words, images, and media. Where are you not being yourself? If you find examples, remove that content and make a commitment to yourself to move forward differently.

Be authentic in your communication so people can see who you are at the core. It's who and what you are at the core that makes the difference.

2

THINK BEFORE YOU POST

In social media (and everywhere else), sometimes it's easy to lose ourselves in the chatter and fast-paced reality that swirls around us. The world of social media moves quickly, and with friends posting information every minute and brands trying to sell to us everywhere we look, it's easy to become frustrated or overwhelmed with the abundance of information and communication that is thrown in front of us.

Instead of jumping in immediately and allowing yourself to get frustrated, take some time to connect with who you are before you engage in the social media conversation.

Many people have regretted what they've posted because they reacted in anger or frustration. Just as with face-to-face communication, once words are out there, they can't be taken back. In fact, on social media, they can spread like wildfire. Just because you delete them doesn't mean they haven't done damage.

So just as you consider the words you speak, consider the words you post. They have an impact that reaches much farther than you think.

Action: Before you post any content online, remind yourself to take ten seconds to read through what you are going to post. Say it out loud, and see how it feels. If it evokes any negative thoughts or emotions, don't post it.

Just as you consider the words you speak before you say them, consider the words you post before you post them.

3

LIKE IT

It sounds simple, right? One little action, one press of the button. It's an easy thing to do, and its reach is much greater than we likely imagine.

What does it really mean when we like something? Well, it means many different things to different people at different times. The only thing consistent is that it means something good.

It can mean any of the following:

- Yay!
- Congratulations!
- I'm proud of you.
- What a great picture.
- I'm glad to share this with you.
- I'm so sorry for your loss.
- I'm here for you.
- I agree.
- I support you.
- I share in your pain.
- I love this.
- I love you.

...or so much more.

Think of what it means to you and how you feel when it happens for you. You've posted something special or shared a picture, and you get dozens of likes from your friends. It's not about how many there are, but rather the feeling of friendship and support that those likes convey.

Likes also bring us closer together somehow. In that moment, when you see the names of friends who have liked your post, it's as if they are there with you, sharing in your life, even from very far away.

When you consider it like that, something as simple as a like can actually create a very profound connection between people.

So when you scroll through your own newsfeed, consider what your likes might mean to your friends. When you want to make sure your friends know that you're there with them in the moment, like their posts. And remember: like it because you mean it.

Perhaps a like on Twitter doesn't do as much as it does on Facebook or Instagram. But those hearts sure are cute! ♡

Action: As you scroll through your social feeds, don't just be an onlooker. If something holds meaning for you or if you want to be supportive, click that like button.

4

USE REACTIONS

Want to one-up your like? Show a greater range of emotion when you can. Although it may seem odd, those signs of emotion convey meaning and make a difference.

Facebook now makes it easy for us to select various reactions: love, sadness, laughter, surprise, and anger.

You should know that these reactions do not just convey meaning to those whose posts you're reacting to. Your reactions also tell Facebook how much you *really* like something, and this impacts how content is shown in your feeds.

So choose your reactions wisely.

Action: Be mindful that reactions will impact what you see in the future. If you really like something and want to see more of that type of content, give it some love, laughter, or wow. If you are actually reacting in anger, consider whether you really need to react at all or if you would be better served by stepping away.

5

STEP OFF THE LECTERN

Social media gives each of us a voice. However, if you're only listening to your own voice, after a while you'll be the only one.

People engage on social media because they want to connect with people. They want to share thoughts and ideas and keep in touch with friends. They want to foster relationships with people over distances and share meaningful experiences that show who they really are.

They want to do that with you.

If you don't actually want to engage with others—to have those conversations, like your friends' meaningful photos, enjoy the humorous videos, or post a supportive comment when they need one—then what are you really doing there?

Friendship goes two ways. So does social media.

Have conversations and enjoy the ones you have.

Action: Look at your social media feeds and notice how much you're posting, commenting, and engaging with others. If you're mostly just posting your own content, make a point to scroll through your friends' posts. See what they're up to and allow yourself to absorb the potential for using social media to lift up your friends and support them. Look for opportunities to engage with your friends and act.

It's not through posting or building contacts but through engaging in social media that the magic truly happens.

6

STEP AWAY

Sometimes only by stepping away from the world of social media can you do good.

Being authentic and real doesn't necessarily mean that you show everything that's going on inside you at every minute with everyone out there in social land.

Would you do that in the offline world? If you're angry at your boss, do you yell and scream at her in the office? If you're upset with your partner, do you post it on a bulletin board so the entire town can share in your momentary misery? Likely not, probably because you realize that it won't do you or anyone else involved any good by handling conflict in a public way. And, in fact, it could cause harm.

So why, then, would the results be any different if you post online?

The truth is that in that moment, if you turn to social media to vent frustration, you're likely not being true to yourself at all. And later, you'll regret it.

So remember: while it is always best to be yourself (online and off), sometimes you can only do that by turning the computer off.

Action: Check in with yourself before you post something online. If you are angry, especially toward someone else, do not post anything. If you are unsure, read your post out loud. If it does not give you a sense of peace, put your device down, and do not post something you may later regret.

If you wouldn't want it on a billboard for the whole world to read, including your grandmother, then it doesn't belong on social media.

7

BE SAFE ON SOCIAL MEDIA

Learning to protect yourself on social media and teaching your children to do the same is one of the very best things you can do for yourself if you are going to spend time online. And let's be honest, aren't we all?

Unfortunately, most adults have absolutely no idea what to do when it comes to protecting themselves. That also means that there are few people teaching young people what they need to know.

Every social media channel has ways in which you can increase your privacy on that network. This is true for some much more than others. The first step, then, is to educate yourself about how to keep your accounts as private as possible and to follow the necessary steps to maximize your privacy. Here are sites with tips to get you started:

- https://www.facebook.com/about/basics
- https://about.twitter.com/safety/families
- https://help.instagram.com/154475974694511
- https://www.snapchat.com/safety
- https://help.pinterest.com/en/help-topic/Safety%20and%20standards

Besides knowing how to protect yourself and your children

on the platforms you use, here are some best practices to follow anytime you are online:

- Turn your locations visibility off.
- Create strong passwords.
- Consider using a nickname when possible. This is especially important for young people.
- Do not share your contact information publicly.
- Never publicize your address.
- Do not tag yourself or friends in photos. When you do, those photos of you then become discoverable when people search your name.
- Never say when you (or family members) are and are not going to be home.
- Keep your social accounts separated (not linked to each other).
- Do not log into other apps using your social media accounts.
- Delete your browsing history regularly.

Also, remember that you do not need to be friends with everyone who requests it. There are ways to report users who are violating your privacy.

By understanding the rules on the social networks we use and by taking the initiative to protect ourselves and our children, collectively, we make the world a safer place...even online.

Action: Take every action you can, starting with the ones listed above, to keep your social accounts private and protect yourself online. Then teach your children to do the same.

8

ENGAGE WITH THE UNIVERSE

What if every day you could tap into the power of the universe to remind you what a beautiful human being you are? And what if every day you could share that message with the world through social media?

As it turns out, you can.

The Universe, otherwise known as Mike Dooley, sends out "Notes from the Universe" on a daily basis, along with other uplifting and inspiring content designed to raise our vibrations and bring happiness to the world. You can read these notes on Facebook, Instagram, or Twitter, and you can also subscribe at Tut.com to have them emailed to you or download the app to have them delivered to your phone.

I've done all the above.

Reading and sharing the most recent "Note from the Universe" as part of my daily routine helps me stay positive about myself and all that I have to offer in life. Here some of my favorite nuggets of wisdom from The Universe:

- "Thoughts become things. Choose the good ones."
- "Can you imagine the joy, the peace, the complete sense of satisfaction? The harmony, the live, and stitches of laughter? Can you imagine the interest income?! Good, because nothing else shapes mountains, people, and bank accounts quite like imagination."

- "As surely as the snow falls, the winds rage, and the rivers run, so are you, minute by minute, day by day, inevitably drawn to all your heart desires. Act on this."
- "Reframe every thought, word, and action from the perspective of the person you've always dreamed you'd be, as if your life was already as you've always dreamed it would be."
- "You want what you want because you know it's possible. If it wasn't, you wouldn't. This is powerful. Embrace it. For whatever else you believe or don't believe, this belief alone can take you the distance." [1]

Give yourself the gift of engaging with The Universe. Then share that gift with others.

Action: To lift yourself up on a daily basis, like and follow Mike Dooley—The Universe on social media, and subscribe to his daily "Notes from the Universe." You'll be forever grateful.

9

CELEBRATE BIRTHDAYS

Every day we wake up is a day to celebrate life and what we are creating for ourselves. Birthdays, however, are the one day each year when everyone else gets to wake up and celebrate us, too.

Now, the advent of social media has made it possible for you to share that day with friends and family far and wide. I think we can all be honest in saying that this is a great feeling. Whether you see your birthday wishes on the day or you check the next day and find them, those wishes are affirmations that people around us care about us and are thinking about us on that day.

This can be a reconnection time. Maybe you haven't heard from certain friends in a long time, maybe a year even. But when you get that happy birthday wish, they're there with you, at least for a moment. In some ways, it's like a big party just for you.

Keep that in mind when your friends' birthdays come along. Remember how nice it feels to have someone post those two simple words: happy birthday.

Or you can give your wishes a twist. Social media abounds with humorous and sentimental birthday wishes that stray from the norm. In fact, Birthday Wishes Expert has compiled some of the more original birthday greetings, so you can copy them and post them on social media yourself.

For example, consider the following:

- Happy Birthday! Thanks for always being older than me.
- I love you, but don't push your luck. I know your real age. Happy Birthday!
- Everyone is inscribing great birthday wishes on your wall today. I certainly can't be left out. Happy birthday, long life and prosperity. [2]

Birthday Wishes Expert has a humorous collection of birthday memes, as well. [3]

And some favorites from my own birthday wishes:

- Happy birthday, gorgeous!
- You are loved. You are missed. But most of all I hope you are blessed.
- Wait, didn't you have a birthday last year?
- Here's to a day filled with spectacular moments.
- Dananananana, they say it's your birthday, so happy birthday!
- My life would have gone in all different directions if I had not met you.
- You're like sunshine and warm chocolate chip cookies right from the oven. Happiness.
- Get spoiled!
- Happy birthday to the awesomest person ever.
- Wishing you a day as fabulous as you are.

Action: Take the extra few seconds and post happy birthday wishes to your online friends. It will warm your heart and theirs.

10

GIVE QUICK WARNINGS

Social media is one of the best places to warn your local friends about things that have happened in the moment that they need to know about ASAP.

For example, is there a big accident on the highway that has traffic backed up for hours? The first absolute rule is: don't post while you're driving. However, if you are the passenger, take a moment and let people know to avoid that route.

This can save your friends a lot of time and help cut down on traffic in the area.

Is there bad ice on a bridge or flooding on a low-lying road? Once you get through it safely and are off the road, tweet it or quickly post on Facebook...wherever your friends are most likely to see it.

Is there a break-in or other crime that just occurred? Get yourself to a safe place and then make sure other people know so they can stay clear or take whatever precautions they need to in order to protect themselves.

In these instances, the purpose isn't to spread panic. So make sure to avoid sensationalism and just report the quick facts that will help your friends avoid dangerous or difficult situations in local areas.

Action: Know that people may view your social media posts sooner than they do announcements on traditional news networks. Be the newscaster when you need to be; just make sure you are safe first before you do so.

11

SIGN ON THE (VIRTUAL) DOTTED LINE

If you want to magnify your voice for change, starting or signing petitions is a powerful way to do so. Rather than going door to door, we can now gather support via social media.

Change.org is one organization dedicated to supporting people around the world in their efforts to make change at local, national and global levels.

"On Change.org, people connect across geographic and cultural borders to support causes they care about." [4]

To date, more than 214,000,000 people have taken action by signing petitions, and those signatures have led to more than 24,000 victories in almost 200 countries.

All of the petitions on Change.org are started by individual users and published on the open platform. If you're ready to put your voice to work supporting issues you believe in and making change, lend your virtual signature and then share the petitions online so that others can do the same.

Action: Don't keep your causes a secret. The next time you believe strongly enough in something to sign it, take the time to share it on your social channels.

Together we have the power to inspire, to shape our futures, to change the world. We may yet discover that social media is the most powerful way to do just that.

12

KEEP RELATIONSHIP UPDATES OFFLINE

If you and your friend, boyfriend/girlfriend, family member, or partner have a fight, do you call the local news station and let them know? Likely not. That's pretty much the equivalent of posting it on social media. In posting what's happening in your relationship, you're sharing everything with the world…the good, the bad, the ugly, and often the hurtful.

Posting about your relationships isn't just about you. While you may need to let off steam, making a public declaration about your relationship doesn't just affect you. It affects the person you are posting about as well as the people who care about you both.

While your relationship might heal, you can never take away the fact that you posted about it online. You may delete the post, but the damage has been done. The trust has been broken.

If you need to share what's happening, do it. Pick up the phone. Call a friend. Talk about what you need to talk about. Just think long and hard about the long-term consequences of posting it on your social channels.

Action: When you're feeling the emotional impact of a relationship change, step away from social media. Reach out to your friends and have one-on-one, private conversations that will give you the personal support you need.

13

DON'T JUST TELL...SHOW

Thinking back to language arts since grade school, teachers have been telling us to show instead of tell. Social audiences want to see, not only read.

That's why images and multimedia content are met with such success. Visual content draws people in and helps them to share in an experience on a deeper level.

And then there are Pinterest and Instagram—social networks completely devoted to empowering us to *show* what we love through visuals.

Pinterest boards and Instagram feeds are like dessert for visual ideas. So very yummy.

Why not serve up some dessert? See something you love? Experience the best-tasting meal ever? Find a great new recipe? Did you single-handedly figure out how to solve your child's bedroom/desk organization? Brilliant. Snap it. Post it. Pin it.

If you love the idea, whether or not you came up with it yourself, someone else will also love it and be so very grateful to you for showing them how to do it, too.

Action: Don't just tell the world what you love...show it.

14

AVOID FAKE NEWS

Unfortunately, there are many influencers (both individuals and organizations) who choose to influence using "information" that is not entirely (and sometimes not at all) accurate. There are even more social media users who perpetuate the believability of this inaccurate information because they believe it to be news instead of what it is—subjective propaganda. There's not one belief system or political agenda for which this is true more than others. It's true across the board.

Fact-check your news, people. Don't unknowingly perpetuate lies and be part of the problem.

Do yourself and everyone else good. Find out the truth. Go to resources like Snopes or at least ensure that the same information you're seeing is consistent across multiple highly credible sources. [32]

Keep in mind that not all news sources are equal. Also keep in mind that just because it's a famous news source, its information may not always be right.

We are living in an information age, and more people get their information from social media than from any other source.

Be part of the movement that stands for sharing truthful news with the world…and speak out when you see fake news being perpetuated.

Action: Check the facts before sharing or commenting on "news" stories on social media. Make sure the sources are reputable, and check to see if the same information can be confirmed from multiple highly respected sources. Not sure where or how to check the facts? Snopes is a great place to start.

We are living in an information age, and more people get their information from social media than from any other source. Be part of the movement that stands for sharing truthful news with the world.

15

REMEMBER YOUR CHILDREN WILL GROW UP

Note: While all the remarks I'm about to make are directed to parents with children, keep in mind that this all holds true for adults and adult behavior.

So many parents get super excited about sharing pictures of their kiddos, and rightly so. However, sometimes this can be taken too far. I'm not referring to the number of photos, necessarily, but rather the content of the photos. Posting photos that may now seem "cute" to other parents but will later be very embarrassing to teenagers and young adults may not be the best strategy. Consider these situations for example: bath time, during tantrums, during a crisis, and so on.

This holds true for adults, too. Posting what might be considered as compromising photos of your friends at inopportune times serves no long-term positive value.

It's important to remember that social media has a long memory. Even if you think the social platform you're using is private, it isn't. Those photos may well wind up on Google, especially if you have named your child in the post.

Also, take care in posting anything that is overly personal about your child: birthdate, age, school, and so on. This simply reveals too much information that could come back to haunt you and them in the future.

Be proud. Share those moments that you love. Just remember that what you share will one day represent your grown child, too.

Action: Before you post photos of your children, consider the impact these photos could have on them in the future.

16

BE UPWORTHY

The inspirational videos produced and shared by Upworthy are often just the pick-me-up we need. Sometimes they're the thoughtful prodding that causes us to take action. Other times they bring much-needed comic relief.

In all cases, they are aimed at helping us pay attention to what's really important in life "because we're all part of the same story." [5]

Upworthy's mission is "to change what the world pays attention to. [They] believe that stories about important issues can and should be great stories—stories for everyone, stories that connect us and sometimes even change the world." [5]

That is a worthy mission, indeed.

Consider the positive impact it has when we seek out these kinds of stories and share them with others. In doing so, each of us can be a vehicle for transformation. We can help narrate the collective human story.

Action: The next time you're looking for a great story to inspire yourself and others, see what Upworthy has to offer, and pass it on.

17

FRIEND AUTHENTICALLY

Not everyone on Facebook or any other social platform needs to be your friend. Some platforms don't allow us much choice for accepting friends. However, on the ones that allow you to choose to accept friends or connections, choose carefully. Some are more private in nature than others.

For example, if you are using social media for business, LinkedIn is likely a place where you can safely accept most connection requests. However, if there is no photo, no real name, and no common connections, perhaps it is worth a second thought. If the connection request comes with an appeal for help with transferring international funds or with an unsolicited romantic advance, the best response is to ignore the request and perhaps ban the pursuer if the requests continue.

If you are using Facebook for business, consider carefully whether you want to accept business contacts as personal friends. This can be a huge benefit to business. However, it also means that your business connections are seeing everything you post. You may want to limit the personal nature of your posts in this instance.

This "rule" is even more important for young people. It is so important for teenagers to understand that they do not have to and should not accept every friend invitation they receive. While it's not nice to think about, the reality is that there are predators, both young and old, whose friend requests should be denied at all costs.

Do good for yourself by saying yes to the right connections and no to the wrong ones.

Action: Consider each connection request carefully before saying yes, and don't accept requests from anyone whose trust you question. Teach your children to do the same.

18

SMILE WHILE YOU POST

Now, this one probably sounds silly, doesn't it! How could you do good by smiling? Well, the truth is that you could do a lot of good.

Have you ever been out walking around and seen someone smiling, looking happy, and then started smiling yourself? Or have you realized that you're the one smiling and that you're having an impact on others?

Smiles are contagious, and believe it or not, they can be transmitted in many ways, not just in person. You can hear a smile over the phone. It changes the tone of a conversation. You can also see smiles through social media posts. If you smile when you're posting something, the words you choose will reflect that. If you're sad or angry, your words will reflect that. Similarly, if you're just posting to impress others, you will come across as insecure.

This isn't to say that you won't be able to fool some people. You will. But why? Why try to fool anyone?

If you aren't truly happy and can't smile while you're posting, then consider whether you really need to be posting anyway. (Maybe you do, maybe you don't…just take a minute to think about it.)

As the old familiar song goes, "If you're happy and you know it, clap your hands."

Maybe clapping your hands isn't necessary. A smile, on the other hand, is transformative for you and for everyone who shares in your smiling posts.

Action: Smile as you are sharing content on social media, and your smile will create a ripple of smiles that will keep going.

19

ANSWER QUESTIONS

Social media provides many opportunities to share your knowledge, show your expertise, and share your opinion.

People actively use social media to search for solutions they need. They ask for recommendations and input on every subject imaginable, from professional to personal and sometimes just for fun.

The next time a friend asks a question, don't just scroll past if you have an answer. Share yours.

This is an opportunity to showcase your expertise if you have professional advice to offer. It is also a chance to support businesses you love or share favorite things.

Keep in mind that there may be different opinions and recommendations shared, so this is also an opportunity to learn from different perspectives.

Action: If you know an answer or have an opinion when you see a question asked on social media, share what you know.

20

SHARE WHAT IS MEANINGFUL

If something strikes you and has meaning, share it. You can share it with your friends or your business connections. You can also share it with groups or in private messages. Depending on the content, determine the best way to spread the word and get it out there.

If a post resonates with you or is meaningful, don't keep it to yourself. Perhaps it makes you laugh. Perhaps it touches your heart. Perhaps it just hits close to home, and you know your friends will know exactly why you're sharing it and who it's for.

Chances are very high that if a post or tweet means something to you, it will mean something to your friends.

The same holds true for business. If it has the potential to make a positive impact on your business, surely it can positively impact other businesses as well. If it is relevant to your businesses, your colleagues will find it relevant, also.

Social media isn't for secrets, so spread the great content around.

Action: When you come across content that is meaningful to you, take the time to share it with others.

21

COMMENT AND REPLY

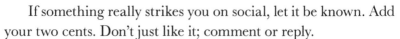

If something really strikes you on social, let it be known. Add your two cents. Don't just like it; comment or reply.

The comments and replies are what turn content into conversation. They are what strengthen relationships. They are the building blocks of great stories, and they happen thousands and thousands of times every day.

A funny post, an inspiring post, a helpful post, all those do good on their own. With likes and retweets, they spread and make an impact. However, with comments and replies they can become that much funnier, more poignant, more meaningful and more beneficial to others.

They can also forge strong connections between people, and the virtual conversations they spawn are real, personal and meaningful to the ones participating and to witnesses taking it all in.

So, if a post really speaks to you, if a response comes to mind while you're reading it, then assuming your response is something that will build up conversation not tear it down, don't keep that response to yourself.

Action: Participate in conversations on social media and share your thoughts by commenting on the posts of others.

22

BE CONSTRUCTIVE IN SHARING DISLIKES

If you don't like something, should you say it or not? Should you announce it to the world or keep it to yourself? Can it really do good on social media by sharing content about something you've come to recognize as bad?

Here's the thing. If you have a chance to stand up against something you think is wrong, and your voice has the opportunity to make a difference, speak up. You're being true to yourself and staying committed to what you believe in.

Even smaller such issues can impact people's lives for the better, like discovering something about a type of food that's harmful. You've done your fact checking, and you know that everyone should have this information in hand to make the right choices. By all means, share away. However, do so in a way that is constructive and positive rather than belittling, accusatory or negative.

There are also some dislikes that almost never have a place on social media. For example, if you don't like a certain person right now—your partner, your boss, your former BFF—vocalizing that dislike on social won't result in any positive impact. It could come back to bite you (HARD) later, and you'll often live to regret it.

Action: If you need to share a dislike on social media, make sure you have checked your facts first and then share your information in a constructive and positive way to help others.

23

AVOID THE FAKE PERFECT PHENOMENON

Life is messy. While we might all like to have Mary Poppins's "practically perfect" life, it simply isn't so. So why fake it? When you consistently post bragging rights that feel just like that, a little too braggy to be real, what are you really trying to accomplish?

Social media isn't about being perfect; it's about being real, being yourself. It's about having the opportunity to stay connected with people who would otherwise be too far away to stay in touch in a consistent way. It's not about having to be perfect all the time.

That's not to say, however, that it's a forum for complaining either. No one wants to hear that, and that just brings other people down. However, hopefully it can be a place where you truly can share who you are with your friends. Otherwise, why are they your friends anyway?

Now, I'm not suggesting that you stop posting all those happy moments. However, if you ever feel like you have to one-up your friends with another post about how awesome your life is from top to bottom, then maybe you're doing it for the wrong reasons. Maybe it just might have a negative impact on the friends you want to be there with you in the first place.

Action: Before you post that next perfect picture, consider why you're posting it and if it's really you being you or if it's you showing off. If it feels like the latter, don't post it.

Social media isn't about pretending to be perfect. There's no right way to be on social media other than to be yourself.

24

LEARN

Social media is like a worldwide online classroom. We now have access to so much knowledge at our fingertips, and often there is no cost attached. It's a portal to free education.

Students who are struggling in their classrooms can access many different approaches to teaching them the same subject matter along with multimedia tutorials to help them learn.

Professionals seeking to strengthen their skillsets can identify training opportunities and follow industry experts.

We can learn everything from cooking styles to repair and installation to makeup and hair design tips…and everything in between.

If you have a question, you can ask your friends. If you need expert advice, you can seek out experts. You can also simply type what you need to learn about into a social network's search bar.

However, proceed with caution. Not everything you read on social media is true. If it's facts you are looking for, check your facts before you trust what you read as true. If the information is accurate, you should be able to find the same information on multiple sources. You can also use a resource like Snopes to check your facts. [32]

The wealth of the world's knowledge is truly at your fingertips in our social world. Be active in discovering the information that you seek.

Action: When you are seeking certain knowledge, make use of social media resources that are available.

25

MENTION AND TAG

Has a friend done something very kind for you? Did you experience great service at a new restaurant? Did you just hear a powerful speaker? Are you attending a great event that is impacting your life right this instant?

Tell people about it. Mention your friend or that restaurant that you love. Tag that speaker or the organization putting on the fantastic event.

These practices do good in many different ways.

First, they tell your friends that they're appreciated, that you care about them, and that you're grateful for the friendship.

They also let all your friends know where they can get great products and fantastic service, while you support the growth of local businesses.

Mentioning and tagging great speakers or other public figures simultaneously shares inspiration and motivation with your network and helps promote those leaders whom you respect so much.

The same is true for organizations and events. You can support the initiatives and benefit your network with the information they offer, all at the same time.

Some great experiences are meant to be kept to yourself. Many, however, can be shouted from the rooftops and, in doing so, impact many. While most of us won't actually get out the ladder to climb onto the roof and shout the news, mentioning and tagging accomplishes the same thing.

Action: Make use of the tagging features on social media to let the world know about greatness happening around you.

26

CLICK A LINK

How can clicking a link do good? Well, it depends on the link.

If your friend or someone in your network has shared a link, clicking on it can do many things: make you laugh, make you smile, make you cry, make you think. These are all good things, assuming the crying is the make-you-feel-good-in-the-end kind of crying. You know the kind I mean.

Clicking on a link also supports the organization or initiative being shared in the link. It takes you back to their website where you can find out more about them and perhaps share their content yourself.

In some cases, clicking on the link enables you to offer direct support to the friend or connection who shared it. It could be your friend's recent blog or video, a piece of news they are really excited about, or a feature that was done about them in a local or nationwide publication.

Clicking on the link is the first step to finding out why this was shared, and then it's up to you to take it from there. You can like it, comment on it, or even share it again yourself. And if the link wasn't that great, you can leave well enough alone.

You won't know what you want to do, however, until you click the link.

Action: The next time you see a shared link that piques your interest, click on it to find out more. In contrast, if you see a link that appears in some way offensive to you, don't support it by clicking on it.

27

USE EMOJIS

Don't emojis make you want to smile? Well, either that or you want to poke your eyes out.

If you fall into the former category, you're one of millions who love, love, love to add a bit of flair to their posts using the ever-popular emojis.

With emojis we can personalize our posts and add a bit more emphasis to the emotions we're trying to convey. We can make a virtual hug, kiss, or smile that much stronger. Plus, we can momentarily get back in touch with our inner child and have a bit of fun.

Go on. Try it the next time you post something on social. I bet it will make you smile.

Action: When you need to add some emotional emphasis, have some fun playing with emojis. Just keep in mind that not all of them are the feel-good kind.

28

BEWARE SHARING TOO MANY SELFIES

Selfies have become one of the most popular and most common ways for us to express ourselves. Why? Because we're able to capture ourselves in the moment of an experience that we want to share with others.

Selfies can be silly or serious; they can be with others or alone. They can be mirrors into who we are, and they can be lots of fun.

However, *too many* selfies can be something else.

It's a bit like someone who simply talks about himself or herself and no one else...*all the time.*

It may come across as arrogant even if you don't mean it that way.

It may convey to others that you're not really there to engage with them or have conversations with them but that you're really only there for yourself.

People may unfollow you. You may lose friends.

If you find that more of your posts are selfies than anything else, it may be time to consider whether your social media use is really just about you...and whether you want it to stay that way.

Action: Consider how you use selfies as part of your social media use to make sure your conversations aren't just one-sided photo bombs of you. Use selfies to capture special moments rather than to put yourself on display.

29

TEDIFY YOUR SOCIAL MEDIA

TED Talks offers videos on pretty much everything under the sun. If you're looking for information or inspiration, you can find it there. And when you do, share it with others. It will make a difference in someone's day…you can count on it!

I've been enlightened, inspired and moved to tears watching TED Talks. Here are some of my favorites:

- "Every Kid Needs a Champion"—Rita Pierson
- "My Year of Saying Yes to Everything"—Shonda Rhimes
- "I Got 99 Problems…Palsy Is Just One"—Maysoon Zayid
- "The Power of Vulnerability"—Brené Brown
- "Why the Only Future Worth Building Includes Everyone"—His Holiness Pope Francis

Action: Give yourself the gift of time watching TED Talks that are meaningful to you, and share them with others in your network.

30

LIKE A PAGE

How can liking a page or following an organization do good? It supports them, both by showing your support and by literally helping them grow.

Has a friend asked you to like a new business? Are there businesses that you love either for their fabulous products or their top-of-the-line service? Are there organizations that you believe in and want to see succeed?

Well, don't just tell them, "Great job," "Good luck," or "I'm rooting for you." Show them you mean it by supporting them online.

Liking or following an organization online makes a public statement. It puts your support out there for everyone to see (and of course if you share their content, you do even more.)

The only caveat is that you should only like the page if you actually like and want to support the organization. Don't do it just to be nice. The pages you like are a reflection of you, so like a page because you mean it.

Action: The next time you come across a business page or profile you love, click the like button. It's as easy as that.

31

SUPPORT A CAUSE

Social media provides many, many, *many* opportunities to donate to causes that you believe in.

Within any group of friends, there is likely a cause shared relatively often. Whether it's something global like the ALS Challenge or #MeToo campaign, both of which were heard 'round the world, or it's something more personal like a friend's participation in the Race for the Cure, social media provides us with an array of causes to support and an easy process to do so.

Social media makes it easy to click a link, read a story, click donate, and enter payment info, all within a matter of minutes. Then we can support the cause further by sharing it again ourselves, spreading the word and making it easy for others to follow in our footsteps.

Why support a cause? To raise money for research, to increase the likelihood and speed of finding cures, to provide quick relief for those in need, to support our friends in their endeavors to do good themselves. There are an endless number of reasons. Can you support every cause? Absolutely not. Choose the one or ones that are most meaningful for you and then leverage social to multiply the good that you're doing on your own.

With social, we can double, triple, multiply our efforts ten times and more. There are no limits to the reach and the impact when we join together to support the causes that do good.

Action: When you want to lend your support to a cause, share it on social so that others may do the same.

Through social media we have an opportunity not only to make a difference locally, but to impact the lives of people around the world.

32

CRAFTIFY YOUR KID-DOM

While social media isn't a place to be, it is a fantastic place to find ideas for projects, crafts, and other learning activities to do with your kids. Scroll through Facebook pages of organizations like Scholastic or do a general search on Pinterest. You're sure to find something fun for the young'uns to do any given day.

While I am by no means a child-activity expert, here are some of my favorite places to find family-friendly ideas for fun:

- Kid-Activities on Pinterest [6]
- Easy Activities for Kids on Facebook [7]
- Fun Family Crafts on Facebook [8]
- Make and Takes on Facebook [9]
- Quirky Momma on Facebook [10]

Action: Turn to your social media network when you need new ideas for fun and educational ideas for the young (or young at heart) people in your life.

33

SHARE CONTENT FROM NOT-FOR-PROFIT ORGANIZATIONS

If you're ready to take a more active role in promoting the not-for-profit organizations you support, make a point to keep an eye on their social updates. Then share them with your friends and followers.

Whether it's an inspirational photo, a heartbreaking fact, a video that warms your heart, or a call to action, if you believe in it and it holds meaning for you, share it with others.

Sharing inspirational messages from the not-for-profit organizations you support will inspire others. Sharing facts and statistics about their work will educate. Sharing videos that touch your heart will, in turn, touch the hearts of others.

I would caution against only one thing, and that is consistently sharing calls for support and nothing else. If you are regularly asking your friends to make donations, for example, they may eventually unfollow you so they won't see your frequent bids for their pocketbook. Then your efforts are wasted because few people are seeing your shares anyway, and when they do, your shares will have lost their potency because they are so frequent.

Sometimes a more passive approach does more good. Share posts that are most meaningful to you, the ones that made you want to support the organization in the first place. Then let people be inspired, as you were, about the good the organization is doing, and you will see support grow.

Action: When you come across great content in the social feeds of your favorite not-for-profit organizations, share it with others.

34

SUPPORT BUSINESSES YOU BELIEVE IN

If there are businesses you want to support, there's a lot you can do on social to help. Whether it's the local café you frequent for business meetings, the farmer's market you visit on the weekend with your family, a hotel you visit every time you're in town, or a service provider with great customer service, the best way for you to say thank you is to share them with the world.

Here are some things you can do to show your support:

- Like their pages on Facebook and LinkedIn. Follow them on Twitter and Instagram.
- Share their posts when they are ones that entertain you or hold meaning.
- Leave them a great review.
- Give an endorsement.
- When a friend on social is looking for something, tell them what you recommend and tag that business.
- When you visit the business, post photos of yourself there.

You are a powerful advocate for helping businesses to grow. Don't be a silent supporter. Use your voice and be proud to tell people how great they are.

Action: Use your social media accounts to spread the good word about businesses that you love.

35

SHARE YOUR TIPS

Those times when you discover something that saves you a lot of time or cuts down extra work or just something you wish you had known before, share those how-to tips with others. Whether it's a great trick for cleaning ovens or an innovative storage solution or anything else, put it out there. You'll look like the genius that you are, and everyone else will be one tip smarter.

Here are a few of the amazing tips my friends have shared that seem small but pack a big punch:

- Clean your oven glass door with a paste of baking soda and water, leaving it to sit for fifteen minutes before wiping it off.
- If you are told your plane has to be taken out of service for maintenance, call your airline's customer service immediately. Do not wait to find out if the flight will be cancelled.
- Know the difference between the best-before date and the expiration date.
- Use a lingerie bag to wash small items in the dishwasher.
- Eliminate an ant infestation by spraying with vinegar and lemon juice then sprinkling the area with cinnamon.
- If your passport is set to expire in six months, renew it now before you travel.

Action: Share your helpful tips and tricks with your friends online. They'll be as grateful as you were when you discovered it in the first place.

36

DON'T SPAM VIA YOUR MESSAGES ON LINKEDIN

LinkedIn is the largest "professional" social network, and in many ways, it is considered to be the safest. Being such, it makes sense that for many this is a key platform for business development.

However, there are some big no-no's that will result in losing connections pretty fast. One of those is sending bulk promotional emails. These emails are spam. Justify it however you want, and that's still what they are. No one wants to receive impersonal emails soliciting something.

Many network marketers are taught this approach, and many simply see it as a great way to reach the masses with their message. So, you upgrade your LinkedIn account so you can send bulk emails telling everyone about the latest and greatest promotion you have going on.

The thing is that while your connections have agreed to be connected to you, they haven't agreed to receive repeated unsolicited emails from you. The exception is if you're part of a specific group or network and this is how you all have agreed to communicate your messages.

It's off-putting and an invasion of privacy. If you want to build professional relationships, that starts with respecting others.

You'd never meet someone at a networking event and simply

start spouting off promotion…or at least that wouldn't be good business. You'd reach out, shake their hand, and get to know them.

Carry that professionalism through to your LinkedIn emails, and if you want to send emails, personalize them and start a real conversation.

If you feel like reaching the masses on LinkedIn is key to your organization's growth, explore its paid ad and messaging solutions.

Action: Keep your LinkedIn emails personal and aimed at building relationships.

37

UNITE

Whatever you believe in, there are others who believe in that, too. Whatever support you need, there are others who need that support.

Your social media channels are a powerful way to connect with people who share your needs, experiences, values, and so much more. So start looking.

Find those organizations. Join those groups. Have those conversations. Share the content that is meaningful to all of you.

Together you can build a collective voice that supports each other and intensifies your message to the world, if that is your intent. There is strength in numbers. Plus, it always feels good to know you are not alone. And that is the 100 percent truth. You are never alone, even on the days it may feel as if you are.

Action: Turn to your social channels to unite with others who share common needs and interests with you.

38

REALLY MEAN IT

Really mean what? Everything.

When you post something, mean it. Post it from the heart. Stand behind what you say.

When you comment, mean it. When you retweet, mean it. When you share something, mean it. Even when you like something, mean it.

Why? Because if you don't mean it, why are you doing it anyway? And if you're just going through the motions, stop. No one needs you to show up on social media and be there when it's not really you.

If you can't show up and really mean it, for the sake of yourself and everyone else in your networks, don't. Take a minute. Take a day. Turn it off. Step away. (Oh look, it rhymed.)

Take whatever time you need and when you're ready to mean it, come back.

Action: Take action on social media only when it holds meaning for you.

39

LIKE AND FOLLOW YOUR FAVORITE NOT-FOR-PROFIT ORGANIZATIONS

Using your social channels as a way to promote the not-for-profit organizations you believe in is a powerful way to do good. Every like or follow they get increases their visibility. With higher numbers, they get higher reach. And with a higher reach, they can connect with more people who can help them achieve their goals.

Your like or follow is an endorsement of the organization you believe in. It's a way for you to stand up and lend your support. It's such an easy thing to do, and while it may seem small, when it comes to doing good, every small thing counts. In fact, it's most often the small things that matter most.

Your friends and followers will see that you support that not-for-profit, and who knows? Maybe they'll look more closely at what the organization stands for and what good it does in the world. With a simple like or follow, you're spreading the word.

Action: Like and follow the not-for-profit organizations that you want to support.

40

STAY IN TOUCH WITH CURRENT EVENTS

You can bet that whatever is happening in your town or in the world, your friends on social media are talking about it. It's a great way to make sure you're on top of what's going on.

Recently there was a wildfire about twenty miles south of our house. We could see that the sky had become hazy, and a quick look on social media verified the fire, which we then confirmed with a local news source. Often important news like that can be available on social even before it hits the news.

Social media can also bring us all together when we are feeling the impact of local or global events. Whether an event occurs in Paris, New York, or any other city in the world, we can share in those experiences together.

One important word of caution: make sure you do your own fact checking, and stay away from sharing fake news.

Action: Use your social media channels to stay on top of current events, especially things happening in your local area.

41

CELEBRATE SUCCESS

When your friends post something they are happy and proud about on social media, it's because they want you to share in the celebration of that accomplishment. So take them up on the invitation.

While you may not be right around the corner to pop down to the local pub for a celebratory toast, you can easily celebrate with them via social, if nothing else. This could be as simple as a congratulatory reply to their original post. It could be a private message sending them your heartfelt thoughts. It could be a song, a video, a meme, some virtual flowers…whatever feels right for you.

When the occasion is right, this could also mean sharing their accomplishment to help them spread the word. This may not be the appropriate course of action for more personal celebrations like a marriage or a child's birthday. It could be perfect, however, when someone has earned some much-desired recognition or achieved a long-time goal.

If you aren't sure whether something should be shared or not, just ask. Let your friends know that you'd love to share their good news but that you wanted to confirm whether it was okay with them first.

Join in your friends' celebrations one way or another, and know that their joy will be magnified as you do so.

Action: When you see celebratory posts from your friends on social media, take the time to respond in some way and celebrate with them.

In a way, social media has made every moment we live into more of a celebration because we are able to share those moments with others.

42

MAKE YOURSELF AVAILABLE TO OTHERS

Social media is a personal experience. It's about relationships. It's about people. It's about being present as yourself and connecting with those you care about.

That means being there when you are needed.

Many social media users (individuals and businesses alike) see social media as a lecture podium. They stand up, share what they have to say, and leave. In other words, they log onto their social channels, they peek through the social news others are sharing, they post their latest rants, and then they log off. Sometimes they don't even look at their friends' news but rather hop on, post, and leave.

Your friends on social media are your friends because they want you in their lives. They want you to share in their everyday comings and goings, even if you're far away. So that means that you need to be there. You need to make yourself available to your friends.

That begins simply with being present while you're on social media and beginning to see that you are part of a conversation rather than a lecture.

Then it's about recognizing when your friends really need you when you see what they're posting. Once your eyes are open to seeing when they need support and encouragement, it will be easy for you to spot those opportunities.

Respond to their posts or send private messages letting them know that you're there when they need you. The more you participate in these relationships with your friends on social, the more they will be there for you when you need them most.

Action: Participate in social conversations so that you can recognize when your friends need you and reach out to them to give them support.

43

DON'T POST IN ANGER

When you post on social media in anger, the delete button may come too late.

When we're experiencing anger, it's not the time to engage with others. Conversations turn into arguments that rarely get resolved, and we say things we may later regret and want to take back.

But we can't.

Once it's out there, you can never fully take it back. The damage has been done. People have been hurt. And the impact and pain may not stop there.

Find another way to express your anger. Write in your journal, take a boxing class, go for a run. Do whatever you need to do to work through your anger without turning it into a public spectacle.

Posting on social media in anger never leads to anything good, so make a commitment to yourself not to do it.

Action: When you are angry, step away from social media.

Sometimes hitting the delete button is just too little too late.

44

LEAVE YOUR CRANKINESS OFFLINE

We all have those days. Cranky, cranky, cranky.

Whether it starts when you wake up in the morning or is triggered by something during your day, something deep down just isn't all that happy. And instead of being able either to let go or just fake it, you let it steep.

It festers. You stew. And then you just can't hold it in anymore, and your first instinct is to take it out on others.

Do you think anyone wants to be around right then?

No. And really, you shouldn't be around anyone else either... you just need time for yourself.

So take it.

Take the time you need, and put your mobile device down. Because if your crankiness is seeping out in real life, it will seep out on social, too, and you won't be able to take it back.

Not being a crank on social is a true gift to everyone you know and to yourself.

Action: When you're not in a good mood, take time for yourself away from social media.

45

MAKE SOMEONE'S DAY

Every now and then we all have *that* day...that day when we're feeling just blah for one reason or another. Yes, each of us is responsible for getting ourselves out of our own funk. However, it sure can make a positive difference when a friend takes the time to do two things: 1) notice that you're having a blah day, and 2) do something about it.

The awesome thing about social media in this case is that you don't have to be face-to-face or even in the same town or the same country in order to take action and make someone's day.

Instead of bringing over some flowers, Kleenex, and a bottle of wine (which if you are in the same town, please, please do as well), you can reach out in a virtual way.

Some potential ideas:

- An entertaining meme
- A funny e-card
- A Someecard [33]
- A private message letting them know you're there to talk
- A song to cheer them up
- A funny movie scene
- A humorous GIF
- A simple thinking-of-you note

None of these take much time. However, they can have a very

powerful impact on the receiver. They can give the perfect lift to make a blah day very *un*blah.

These social hugs are a great way to reach out to those you care about when they need it most. Of course, sometimes it is always best to pick up the phone, and if you are close by, remember that an in-person hug may be just what the doctor ordered.

Action: Reach out to your friends on social media, and give them the support they need from you.

46

RESEARCH

Because everyone is on social, the answers to everything you need to know are likely right there. Whether you need to do market research, gather data for a project, or something else, social media has a wide range of tools to support you.

Here are some ways to use social media to do research:

- Create a survey, put it out there (to friends, customers, or in special interest groups), and ask the questions you need to have answered.
- Use the various social insights tools to help you gather the data you need. Every platform has a range of tools available, and depending on what research you need to conduct, you may find that one platform will help you more than others. Using these tools, you can target specific demographics to meet your research requirements.
- Need to put together a focus group? Turn to your online networks for participants.
- Just ask. Sometimes you can gather enough of a sample of responses just by asking a single question via your social channels.

There's a lot of data you can gather when you go straight to the source: the people.

Keep in mind that depending on the nature of research

you're conducting, there still may be ethical and methodological standards you need to follow, even on social media.

Action: The next time you need to collect research, consider your social media channels as a potential source.

47

SHARE INSPIRING QUOTES

The spoken and written words of great leaders, philosophers, entrepreneurs, entertainers, and educators often have the power to cut through us right to the core and reach us where it matters most.

They shape our perspectives and challenge us to consider new ideas. They encourage us to embrace ourselves for who we really are and inspire us to dig deep into ourselves and reflect on our greatest purpose.

They give us strength in the face of adversity, and they provide insights into the world's greatest wisdom.

Sometimes, they simply give us the comic relief we need.

In others' words, we often discover parts of ourselves. So, read and share the quotes that inspire you. You never know what discovery might be uncovered from the words you share.

Here are some of my favorites:

- "The future belongs to those who believe in the beauty of their dreams."—Eleanor Roosevelt
- "Opportunities don't happen. You create them."—Chris Grosser
- "If you can dream it, you can do it."—Walt Disney
- "If you don't like the road you're walking, start paving another one."—Dolly Parton

- "Step out of the history that is holding you back. Step into the new story you are willing to create."—Oprah Winfrey
- "What you do makes a difference, and you have to decide what kind of difference you want to make."—Jane Goodall
- "Spread love everywhere you go. Let no one ever come to you without leaving happier."—Mother Teresa
- "The challenge is not to be perfect…it's to be whole."—Jane Fonda
- "Don't look at your feet to see if you are doing it right. Just dance."—Anne Lamott
- "Cherish forever what makes you unique, cuz you're really a yawn if it goes."—Bette Midler

Action: When you come across a great quote, share it on social media.

48

PERSONALIZE LINKEDIN MESSAGES

If you're using LinkedIn at all and are sending requests to people to connect, the best way to do that is by writing a personal message to accompany your invitation.

The default message goes something like this: *Hi. I'd like to connect with you on LinkedIn.*

Now you can also just click the Connect button in many cases and send connection requests without any message at all.

Either option comes across as very impersonal, especially if you want to make an impression. Think of extending your hand to someone when you are first introducing yourself. You don't simply shove it out there and say, "Hi. I'd like to connect with you," or say nothing at all. No, it's more personal than that. It's personal because it's the beginning of a relationship, whatever kind of relationship that may turn out to be.

While LinkedIn is professional, it's personal as well. It's about people building relationships with people.

So when you want to connect with someone on LinkedIn, write him or her a short personal message. You may want to remind the person of where you met. Then be genuine when expressing that you'd like to connect.

Giving your introduction request that personal touch will

make a lasting impression and get your online relationship off to a great start.

Action: When you want to send a connection request to someone on LinkedIn, include a personal note introducing yourself.

49

SHARE WHAT MAKES YOU LAUGH

"Make 'em laugh, make 'em laugh. Don't you know everyone wants to laugh."

Ah, I can hear Danny Kaye in *Singing' in the Rain* now.

Laughter truly can be the greatest medicine, and part of what makes it great is that the dose is different for every person. From campfire jokes to highbrow humor, knock-knock jokes to the *New Yorker*, there's a laugh out there for everyone, just waiting to be experienced and shared.

In saying that, there's also the reality that not *all* forms of humor belong on social media. Some things are best kept for private company.

That still leaves a *huge* wealth of material to play with, and if it brings you a giggle, or a guffaw, let others share in the experience, too.

Just think: if every person on earth laughed at least once a day, surely we would be a transformed society (or many transformed societies). So, what can we do to make that happen?

It's simple. If it brought you laughter, share it with others. When we hold it in, when we don't laugh out loud, when we keep it to ourselves, it's stifling. It's like a constipation of joy. It's time to unblock yourself. Let it out. Laugh. As loud as you can. So everyone can hear it. And share it with everyone you can.

Action: When something makes you laugh, use social media to spread the joy.

50

ENGAGE ON COMMUNITY BULLETIN BOARDS

Social media is often more successful than Craigslist or Kijiji or the bulletin board at your local store for providing opportunities to share announcements or participate in buy/sell/trade opportunities.

This goes far beyond Facebook Marketplace, although I must say I find that a very enjoyable pastime and useful tool. There are many other community groups specific to local interest organizations. This could be anything from moms trading not only goods but also tips and resources to professionals exchanging services.

You may find that a community bulletin board already exists for your local community, and if not, you can start one.

Action: Explore social media resources for engaging in your local community.

51

DON'T BE A BYSTANDER

On social media, as is the case offline, too, there are those occasions when we witness bullying or other harmful abuse taking place. Even on social, it is our responsibility to step up and take action to prevent such actions from continuing.

However, most people do not know where to begin.

The truth is that most social networks have policies and procedures in place to protect users from online abuse. Abusers can be reported to the social networks, for example. Abusers on many platforms can also be blocked.

The first step, however, is to recognize that you have it within your power to do something. Whether the person being targeted is *you* or whether you are witnessing abuse of others, you need to speak out and say something.

Some potential steps for you to take are the following:

- Take screenshots of the communication you see as documentation.
- If you have a personal relationship with the abuser(s), reach out to see if you can open their eyes to recognize that what they are doing is harmful.
- Report the abuser to the applicable social network.
- Report the abuser to authorities if laws are being broken.

- Educate people being abused about how they can protect themselves online or refer them to a resource that can help.
- If the abuser is a student, report the actions to the school.
- If you know the abuser's parents, make them aware of the situation.

Abuse comes in many shapes and forms. Sometimes it falls outside the realm of the law, and other times it doesn't. Regardless of the severity, you do not have to stand by and watch it happen. Take the action you need to protect yourself and the people you love.

Action: When you see online abuse occurring, take immediate action to stop it in its tracks.

52

UNDERSTAND YOUR MOTIVATIONS

Haven't we all had those moments when we look back on what we just said and ask ourselves, "Why did I just say that?" Of course we have.

That same experience happens on social media. We comment without thinking and then realize that wasn't what we intended to say at all. Then we're in a situation where we can delete what we said, but it's already out there and people have seen it. So it can never really be taken back.

Instead, it's important to understand your motivations behind why you want to comment, share, like or retweet something that someone has posted online. Once you understand those motivations, you can then determine the best course of action to follow through.

For example, are you truly happy about something your friend shared, and you want to celebrate with them? Or are you aggravated by the post? In the first case, responding is a great choice. You're happy for your friend and want to show it. In the second case, however, it's best to keep your mouth shut (and your fingers away from the keyboard). If you don't, you'll likely end up taking some action that you regret.

The general rule of thumb is that if you don't have anything nice to say, don't say it. Same goes for social media. So, take the time to consider whether your motivations are positive ones…or not.

Action: Check in with yourself before you engage on social channels, and if you're about to engage for the wrong reasons, don't.

53

AVOID REPLACING FRIENDS WITH PAGE LIKES

I once got a Facebook message from a "friend" saying that she was cutting down her "friend" list, and rather than being friends, she wanted me to like her business page and connect with her that way.

Perhaps it goes without saying that I did not like her business page.

I felt quite snubbed at first. Then after considering it, I realized that had she been a real friend, this wouldn't be an issue…and I don't need non-friends as "friends" on social media.

Nevertheless, she could have handled this in a better way.

There may well be certain social networks that you want to keep for your closest friends and family. However, there are likely other social networks on which you're comfortable connecting personally with your wider circle of acquaintances and colleagues.

For example, LinkedIn is a very trusted professional platform, and users do not engage in the same personal ways there as they do on, say, Facebook. However, it still provides a way for people to stay connected personally and as individuals, which is what we all crave.

I may follow my friends' business pages because I'm interested in what they're doing and want to support their growth. However, that does not take the place of the personal connection I want to maintain with that person.

To honor our relationship, my "friend" could have sent this message:

> *Hi there, I've decided that I'm going to start using Facebook just for personal interactions with my closest family and friends. However, I really want to stay connected, so I'm hoping that we can be friends on LinkedIn instead.*

Having received that message, I would have understood her own personal needs for keeping her Facebook account for her closest friends and I also would have felt that she values our relationship and wants to stay in touch in a different way. That would have left me feeling honored and respected, and I would have gladly honored her needs and connected with her on LinkedIn instead.

So, if you find yourself in that situation, remember that your friends want to be connected with *you*, not just your business. Find a way to make it work so you can maintain those relationships that you value.

Action: Do not remove friends and ask them to like your business page. Instead, offer to connect with them in a personal way on another platform.

54

DEFINE YOUR PERSONAL BOUNDARIES

On social media we can be bombarded with information 24-7 if we allow ourselves to be. We encounter content that inspires us, lifts us up, or makes us laugh, and we also encounter situations that can lead to darkness if we let them. This darkness may be bullying or expressions of negative mindsets or unwelcome romantic advances. It can appear in many forms if we allow it to.

We have a choice.

By defining our personal boundaries, we make conscious choices about what (and whom) we do and do not want to encounter on social media.

This begins with choosing *whom* to connect with and *how* to control our privacy. It then extends to how you choose to engage (*with what* and *with whom*). It also includes *when* you will take action to remove something or someone from your social media world.

When we come face-to-face with those people or situations that make us uncomfortable or attempt to compromise the boundaries we have set for ourselves, we have a choice: stand by and do nothing *or* take action to eliminate that situation.

For example, we are met with different opinions on social on a consistent basis. Some of these opinions can even be offensive. Personally, I almost never unfriend or unfollow people for sharing their beliefs online. However, when people cross the line I have set for myself and use their social space to spread hate, I have chosen to eliminate that hate speech from my social space, and sometimes those people along with their speech. This does not involve bad-mouthing that person or engaging in a public debate. It simply involves me taking the action I need in order to protect my boundaries and preserve my integrity.

What choices do you need to make to preserve your integrity on social media?

Action: Define your personal boundaries on social media, and don't compromise this commitment you're making to yourself.

55

SHARE WHAT MAKES YOU HAPPY

Here's a little song I wrote.
You might want to sing it note for note.
Don't worry. Be happy.

Thank you, Bobby McFerrin, for those timeless lyrics.

This is the greatest gift you can give yourself…the gift of happiness. And when you're feeling it, don't keep it to yourself. Spread the love.

Whether it's a personal moment of joy, an experience that you're proud of, a video that made you laugh, a photo that made you smile, a story that made you cry happy tears, or something else, if it's made you happy, then surely it will bring happiness to others, too.

Sometimes, it's the sharing itself that spreads happiness, even more than the content. Because you took the time to share something that was meaningful to you, that holds meaning for others.

Happiness, like love, becomes magnified when it is shared with others. You don't need a happy challenge, but if that makes it work for you, then go for it. By sharing what makes you happy on social, you impact so many…those close to you and those around the globe.

Before we know it, if we all start sharing our happies, we may just have a happiness epidemic on our hands. Now wouldn't that do some good!

Action: When you have something you're happy about, share it with others.

56

SAY THANK YOU

Two little words. *Big* impact. And the reality is too often they go unsaid.

- When someone wishes you happy birthday, say thank you.
- When someone shares or retweets your posts, say thank you.
- When someone shares some piece of happiness with you, say thank you.
- Say thank you to a restaurant that provided you with great service.
- Say thank you to the mobile service provider that just took care of your problem in less than a few minutes.
- Say thank you to the company that installed your beautiful new floors.
- Say thank you to the school with the best teacher your child has ever had.

We live in a fast-paced world, and too often that means we don't make time for the little acts of gratitude. Saying thank you does so much good, not only for those we are thanking, but for ourselves. A heart of gratitude is one that is open to all the amazing things that life has to offer…all the amazing things we can create for ourselves.

Be thankful for who you are, where you are. Be thankful in

this moment. And when it feels right to you, share that on social… so the world can be thankful, too.

Action: Whenever you have the chance to say thank you on social media, do it.

57

RECOMMEND YOUR FAVORITE THINGS

Stand behind the things you love, and make them public. Tried an amazing new soap? Found a delicious recipe? Had fantastic service at a local restaurant?

Don't keep these things to yourself. Make recommendations by sharing links or writing reviews or creating recommendations. You can also respond with your recommendations when friends are seeking them for specific things.

Taking these steps lets everyone know that you've given your stamp of approval.

When we tell stories about our favorite things and recommend them to others, this leads to respect, trust, and more popularity and growth for whatever that thing is that you're recommending.

If you want to do good for the things you love, whether they're brands, products, places, processes, service providers, or something else, let people know that you love them. People are the best advocates in the world, and your recommendations matter.

Action: When someone is asking for recommendations and you have one, offer your suggestion. When you come across something you love, recommend it to others.

58

AVOID POSTING WHAT COULD HURT SOMEONE ELSE

Now you'd think this would go without saying, wouldn't you? And yet I'm saying it because it does *enormous* good and might perhaps eliminate some of the negative energy that's out there in the world.

Let's be honest and admit that we don't always think before we speak. The same holds true for social media. Often, we post before we really consider whom our words might hurt and how it might hurt them.

A gripe about a coworker or employer, a comment about a "friend" at school, a rant about poor service or unmet expectations, a snide remark about your spouse or partner…while these may feel good in the moment, consider how these might impact others (and yourself) once the moment of anger or disappointment has passed.

Before you post something, put yourself in the shoes of the person who is the subject of your rant. How will that person feel if (when) he or she reads it? Remember: nothing is private. How will you feel when you know that person has read it? Will it solve a problem? Will it lead to anything good?

If not—and especially if these aren't words you would say directly to someone's face—give yourself a few minutes to breathe before you post. You'll be thankful that you did.

Action: Consider whether the words you are about to post will hurt others. If they will, then stop.

59

SHARE INSPIRING IMAGES

> *We are visual creatures. When you doodle an image that captures the essence of an idea, you not only remember it, but you also help other people understand and act on it.* —Tom Wujec

The same holds true for sharing an image on social media.

In the world of social, visual content can make someone's day. It can lead to smiles, laughter, tears, and pure joy. Images can transport you to someplace you've never been and bridge gaps connecting people on one side of the world to the other.

One single image can do so much good. However, since I can't show you my favorite images here, I'll share some of my favorite social channels to visit for visual joy.

- National Geographic (all its variations and channels)
- National.Earth on Instagram [11]
- Inspirational Quotes Hub on Facebook [12]
- InspirationalQu0tes on Instagram [13]
- Ami Vitale (artist on all channels)

In addition to sharing images you find on social, you can also share original visual content. These might be photographs you take yourself or images you create with overlaid text. If you choose to do this, here are some of my favorite image creation tools for social sharing:

- Stencil [14]
- PicMonkey [15]
- Canva [16]

And if you're going to use other people's photos to create your own images, make sure you're sourcing stock photos from a resource like Pixabay [17] or Pexels [18].

Action: Share the images you come across that bring you joy, or create your own and share those too.

60

PLAY

Sometimes a virtual playtime break is just what you need to give yourself a smile. No matter your choice of online fun, you can find something to entertain you when you need a break. Maybe it's playing a game, some window shopping in Facebook Marketplace, or some fun banter with a close friend. Social media provides a wide range of fun to be had by people of all ages.

Of course, there can be too much of a good thing. Remember that social media can be a time suck, so don't let yourself get absorbed into the black hole when there is work to do. Also, remember that social playtime cannot stand on its own. It's important for you to have playtime in the nonvirtual world, too, whether with a good book, a round of golf, a board game or a lunch with good friends.

Action: Enjoy your virtual playtime when you need it, and take the time to enjoy offline fun as well.

61

LOOK UP

More and more often these days, when you go to any social function and look around, what do you see? The top of people's heads. Why? Because their faces are bent down looking at their smartphones.

They're texting, scrolling through social feeds, snapchatting, posting selfies, and more. They're interacting on social channels and yet ignoring the face-to-face social opportunities that are literally right in front of them.

Social media is not a replacement for personal face-to-face interaction. Rather, it's a way for us to extend those interactions when we aren't face-to-face with people: to connect with friends living in other places, to share memories of fun experiences, to continue an in-person conversation and take it to another level.

Social media was never intended to be the sole place where people go to interact with others. And yet, sadly, we see more of this happening every day.

Sometimes the best way to use social media for good is to turn it off for a while, to look around and recognize the opportunities for real connection that are there standing in our paths and to go back to using social media as it was intended…as an extension of our personal relationships, not a replacement for them.

So look up from your smartphone once in a while so you don't let real life pass you by.

Action: Make it a point to schedule time for yourself that is away from social media.

62

WATCH YOUR LANGUAGE

On social media there are literally thousands and thousands and thousands of eyes watching you, every minute of every day. Even if you only have fifty friends, those friends have friends, have friends, have friends. You get the drift.

Seriously, *nothing* is private on social media. Nothing. Really. Do you get it?

So, when you're in a mood and feel like unleashing your aggravation out there for the world to share in your woe, think again. That sh#! could cost you a lot more than you may think.

Your friends' kids could see it. Your kids' teachers could see it. Your boss could see it. Your pastor could see it. Your parents could see it. Whoever you're saying it about could see it. Someone could share it. Someone could take a screenshot of it and share that. Someone could report you. Someone could block you.

You could compromise your reputation. You could lose friends. You could lose your job. The list of potential negative results goes on.

Unfortunately, when it comes to social media, once it's out there, even if you delete it, you can't really take it back. It can never be unseen. This isn't the first time you've read this from me here. Are you starting to believe it?

Consider carefully whether it's worth it to shout that expletive on your social media profile. Maybe—just maybe—you should backspace and post nothing instead.

Action: Avoid using language on social media that could cause damage to you or others.

63

WORK VIRTUALLY

Social platforms can provide great opportunities for virtual work. Whether you choose private groups, live video, chat streams, or something else, there are many online tools that can allow you to flex your workspace every now and then.

As organizations begin to deepen their commitment to corporate social responsibility, they become more aware of the impact our workspaces have on the environment and on personal wellness of employees.

Flexible workspaces save on gas, limit the resources you need to maintain in-house operations, and improve employee health and wellness. Really, you can accomplish your work from anywhere, given the wealth of virtual communication resources at your fingertips.

Just think of the lengthier vacation stays that could take place if you were able to work remotely. Maybe it's something worth pitching to your boss, and if you're an entrepreneur, what are you waiting for?

This concept doesn't only apply to work environments. Students can tap into online tools to work virtually with classmates on assignments and projects, and teachers can use these tools to make it easier for students to access school work from home.

Working virtually, at least on occasion, seems like a win-win for everyone.

Action: Explore ways in which you can incorporate virtual work in your life.

64

AVOID PUI (POSTING UNDER THE INFLUENCE)

There's a reason why drinking and driving is illegal. It's harmful to you and everyone else.

While using social media under the influence can't cause the same kind of damage that driving can, it can still destroy your life.

When we're under the influence, our inhibitions are lowered, and our emotions are heightened. This can be a recipe for disaster. You could easily post something you regret later, and then it will be too late to take it back. This could be something you post directly or a comment you make on a friend's post. Either way, once it's out there, the damage is done.

You could also cause a lot of harm to others. By posting photos of your friends enjoying the party, for example, you are making a choice for them to put their behaviors on public display. Whether they have drinks in their hands or smokes in their mouths or are engaging in overly affectionate displays of passion, it's no one else's place to decide that photos of those things belong on social media.

The repercussions of posting your party photos can be quite serious. It could mean a soured reputation, the loss of friends, the loss of a job, and even, in very serious cases, legal action.

This doesn't mean you should never post at a party. It just means that if you're not in the right frame of mind to determine what should be posted and what shouldn't, then it's best not to post anything at all.

So enjoy your parties. Take lots of pictures. Wait until the next day, and then use your clear head to decide what belongs on social, what gets shared personally with friends, and what gets deleted from the photo vault forever.

Action: When drinking is involved, do not engage on social media.

65

HAVE A FAMILY SOCIAL MEDIA CONTRACT

Social media can be a dangerous place for young people. There are predators and cyberbullies masquerading as their friends, and most often young people do not know how to protect themselves.

However, protecting our youth extends beyond simply teaching them how to set their privacy settings. That's where a family social media contract comes in.

A family social media contract is an agreement created on a foundation of trust within the family. It is intended to create an open environment where everyone in the family can discuss what happens on social media in a nonjudgmental way. It is aimed at encouraging parents to talk with their kids and teenagers to talk with their parents.

A family social media contract might include things like the following:

- What all of you (this includes parents, not just children) will and will not post on social channels
- Shared account access (so that passwords are public within the family)
- Processes of maximizing privacy on all social channels

- Commitment to share with each other any inappropriate activity that takes place (like sexual misconduct or cyberbullying)
- Rules and guidelines for engagement that address everyone's needs so the entire family is in agreement and understands.

It is important for parents to let your kids know that you trust them and simply want to be there when they need you to help keep them safe. It is important for teenagers to let your parents know that you value your privacy and independence on social networks. This can be a great way to keep young people safe while building trust and increasing communication within your family.

Action: If you have children who are old enough to use social media, open the dialogue about creating a social media contract for your family.

66

LEND SUPPORT THROUGH KIVA

By sharing and promoting people and organizations that are doing great things around the world, we can use our social influence to impact lives for the better.

One platform that empowers people to do this is Kiva.

Kiva is a platform where people can donate funds to support people and initiatives all over the world. Their mission, according to their website, is to "connect people through lending and alleviate poverty." [19]

Funds go to people and projects that fall into a number of categories, such as women, refugees, agriculture, entrepreneurship, water and many more. Each of these categories has numerous projects that can be shared on social.

So, if you're looking for a way to increase your impact and spread the word about how others can do the same, check out Kiva. Once you find one that resonates with you, make sure to share it on social.

Action: Explore opportunities to use your social impact for good by supporting initiatives like those showcased through Kiva.

67

KNOW WHEN NOT TO LIKE OR FOLLOW A BUSINESS

As social users, it is common to get requests to like and follow a range of business social media accounts. We get invitations from friends, appeals through email, or tweets asking for follow-backs. Some of these businesses we love and gladly oblige with the requested like or follow. Some, however, we may not wholeheartedly support.

Instead of just liking or following a business page because you're asked to, take some time to consider it first, especially if it's a business you're unfamiliar with or unsure about. Go to their website and find out about them. Learn more about what they do. Is this a business you feel good about supporting, even with something as "small" as a like or a follow?

Think of your likes and follows as an endorsement. On Facebook, your friends see what pages you've liked. Your likes are even used by Facebook as advertising tools. On Twitter, who you follow is public by default. Anyone who can see your profile can see the accounts that you follow. These are a reflection of you, and they make a statement about who you are.

Action: If liking or following a business on social doesn't really feel right, don't do it.

68

ONLY LIKE A POST OR TWEET IF YOU REALLY LIKE IT

Have you ever given the "guilt like"? You tell yourself, *I don't like this, but I really should like it. This person always likes my posts, so I should like theirs.* Wrong!

Liking other people's posts makes them feel good. It also tells them something. It tells them you genuinely enjoyed what they had to say or that you really appreciated their post. It means something, and not just to the poster. It sends a message to everyone else who sees your like.

Your likes are a representation of you. They show parts of who you are. If you're faking it just to "be nice" then you're giving the wrong idea in a lot of ways.

It all comes down to the fact that your social media communication is a reflection of your internal self. So do what you know is right for you.

Action: When you like something, like it. When you don't or just don't care, then don't. It's as simple as that.

69

PAY IT FORWARD

Did the person in front of you pay for your coffee in the fast-food line? Did someone give you his or her leftover tokens for the arcade? Don't you just love reading stories about when those things happen?

I imagine many of you have been inspired by stories of good Samaritans from all over the Internet. I'm sure you've had your own good Samaritan experiences, as well, whether you've been on the giving or receiving side, or both.

I've had the privilege of experiencing both sides of that coin. I've been blessed by strangers who have helped me shovel out my snowed-in car, anonymously paid for my coffee, walked/carried me to safety when I fell and broke my foot…and these are just a few. I'm amazed by the goodness in this world when we open our eyes to see it.

I've also been privileged to give to others. From paying forward a free coffee and arcade tokens to being in the right spot at the right time to help a young pregnant woman find her way home, it's my great honor to give to others when I can.

By sharing these experiences on social media, we inspire others with all the love and joy the experiences gave us. We become part of the movement that's spreading the good news that there are, indeed, many huge-hearted people out there who do "small" acts of kindness that have a *big* impact in the lives of others.

Action: When these things happen in your life, let people on social know. It will inspire many others to pay it forward, too.

70

TAKE CARE WHEN ENGAGING IN ONLINE DEBATE

We've all seen posts from friends or those we follow that just sort of rub us the wrong way. We've seen posts from politicians, musicians, celebrities, and more that we haven't agreed with. Sometimes their posts even infuriate us. However, consider what good will come if you comment back.

I'm not suggesting that you never voice your own opinion. I'm simply suggesting that if your comment is going to spark an online debate, is it worth it?

What good comes of people arguing back and forth on social platforms?

Well, I'd say that depends on the nature of the argument or debate and the way in which it is conducted.

Having discussions, even debates, with people who think differently from us is part of what makes us who we are. It prompts us to consider our own beliefs and think about what we know to be true for ourselves. It also helps us develop our ability to engage in respectful conversations with those who have differing opinions. This is an important skill that all of us would benefit from developing.

So, how does that extend to having debates online? It comes back to the nature of the debate itself. If the debate is good-natured and respectful, then it can be positive. Often, however, people engage before they think and comment in anger or frustration, which leads to arguments that lack respect...arguments that can, in fact, be a very hateful experience for everyone involved.

Avoid those types of debates. Even when someone gets your goat, you're likely going to end up posting something you'll regret later. And then it's too late to take it back.

Action: Before taking up arms in your next social media battle, consider whether this is a respectful conversation worth engaging in and whether your comments can be positioned respectfully, as well. If both of these are not true, it is best to skip the argument entirely.

71

DON'T SHARE PHOTOS OF OTHERS THEY WOULDN'T POST THEMSELVES

Sharing photos is one of the primary reasons why people engage on social media. However, when you start sharing photos of others, consider carefully before you post.

Think about whether the person in the picture would actually post that photo of himself/herself. How do you know? Here are some questions to consider:

- Is it a flattering picture or would the person feel bad about other people seeing it?
- Does it show the person in a good way, or does it show something happening that the person wouldn't want to broadcast? Even a simple glass of wine in hand could be something that person doesn't want to share, or a bathing-suit shot, or a goofy look on the face.

Whatever it is, if posting it could have a negative impact on that person in any way, don't post it. Ask your friends when you take pictures at parties if you can post them. And if you post one and then are asked to take it down, do so quickly and make note of why for the future.

Social media is for strengthening positive connections, and those connections can quickly be ripped apart when trust is lost.

Action: If a photo could potentially have any negative impact on someone else, don't post it. Ask permission first.

72

GIVE A KICKSTART

Believe in something so much you're willing to lend your financial support to its success? Have a great product that needs funding to get off the ground?

Tell others about it. If it's a link to a Kickstarter campaign, that makes it easy. [20]

I've seen crowdfunding campaigns for start-ups including scientific toys, sustainable diamonds, movies, restaurants, and everything in between. My friends Kris Booth, Andrea McCulloch, and Ramona Barckert at Pocket Change Films actually funded their first full-length feature film this way. Before Kickstarter or other online crowdfunding tools had launched, they literally raised pocket change that made it possible for them to make the movie *At Home By Myself…With You*. [21]

Through the power of social media, many projects that otherwise would never have made it can find success through crowdfunding. It's a powerful way for people from around the world to come together and help great ideas become realities.

Action: Whether you're seeking funding for a new venture yourself or excited to support a great idea you've heard about, use the online tools like Kickstarter that are available to you and spread the word.

73

SEND PERSONAL MESSAGES

The art of letter writing isn't dead. The medium has just changed. So while fewer and fewer of us send out the annual Christmas card greeting, that doesn't mean we can't stay personally connected to the ones we love.

One way to do that is to use the social channels at our disposal and send personal messages when we're thinking of friends and family that we love.

In no way am I saying you shouldn't pick up the phone. Please, pick up the phone. And if it calls to you, most certainly write the letter. Holding a piece of personal mail in your hand is still one of the greatest feelings on earth.

However, in today's fast-paced and highly electronic world, sometimes we don't take the time to send the snail mail, and sometimes we don't even take the time to have the one-on-one phone conversations that we really want to.

So, in those between times when you still want to connect, reach out. Let your friends know that you're thinking of them, that you love them. Send them Facebook messages, for example, and tell them how you really feel.

Don't just post on their walls or send them a quick tweet. Take just a bit more time out of your day to spread the love. You'll feel good, and so will they.

Action: Take advantage of the message tools available on the social networks you use to reach out personally to friends.

74

SHARE HELPFUL INFORMATION

Whether you realize it or not, every day there are tidbits of information you have that can benefit others. This may be information that stems from some innate part of you. This may be knowledge you have gleaned during the course of your day. This may be some deep piece of wisdom that you've just come to recognize about the world or the people in it.

It might be an article that you've read that relates to your field. It could be a new recipe that was a huge hit with the family. It might be a new gardening practice, a household cleaning tip, a cooking technique, a new method for tying back your child's hair, or a photo from Pinterest that shows the best way that you've ever seen to organize your bathroom.

Whatever the case, when you come across knowledge you know will benefit others, share it. Learning and sharing knowledge is a key part of how we grow.

Social media can spread knowledge faster than almost anything these days. Pretty soon we'll all be scholars if we just stop keeping it all to ourselves.

Action: Use your social networks to share knowledge that you know will be valuable to those in your network.

75

BOOST YOUR PLN

Social media offers a powerful and far-reaching professional learning network (PLN). Whether you take part in topic-specific Twitter chats, curate content from professionals you respect, or join groups for more in-depth conversations, every social platform offers a range of opportunities for you to build and engage with your PLN.

LinkedIn simplifies this with their group features, making it easy to connect with professionals near or far in most every field. Many industries also use Facebook groups to help professionals stay connected. On both LinkedIn and Facebook, you can search for public groups related to your professional skillset and request to join.

On Twitter, some organizations have public lists that increase the potential for industry connection, and hashtag searches can be extremely useful when searching for those whose tweets you want to engage.

Be proactive about searching for these networking opportunities, and you'll find many powerful resources for professional development literally in the palm of your hand.

Action: Make use of the resources available through your social networks in order to grow your PLN.

76

SHARE A FAVORITE RECIPE

We've all seen fun recipe videos as we scroll through our friends' feeds. Now be honest…how many of you stop and watch and think, "Yum, I want to make that!"

I know I have, and I'm always happy afterward. Sharing a fun recipe is a simple way to brighten someone's day. It offers a new cooking idea, accompanied by a smile.

If you have some trusted favorites, why not share a photo of your recipe card? Or better yet, take a video while you make the dish yourself. You can also turn to Pinterest boards for inspiring ideas and share those. And then there are the mouth-watering recipe videos we have all come to know and love from sources like these:

- Tasty [22]
- Delish [23]

If you're looking for something on the natural and healthy side, my favorite food blog of all time is Simple Balance by Wendy McCallum. You can search her website or find her on Facebook under Simple Balance: Real Food Nutrition. [24]

She shares pictures of her recipes that are easy to make, and it is food your family will love.

Hint: Search for her Triple Chocolate Cookies. You'll thank me later.

See what I just did there? I shared my favorite recipe source... and a favorite recipe.

Now it's your turn.

Action: Share your favorite recipes on social media. If you love them, others will too. And let's be honest: good food makes us happy.

77

SERVE UP SOME SOUL FOOD

Soul food on social media? Indeed. SoulPancake, to be exact. SoulPancake is a mission-driven video publisher, and as their slogan says: "We make stuff that matters." On their Facebook page, they describe their mission, saying, "Our mission is to open hearts and minds through smart and hopeful content that uplifts, inspires, and helps us all figure out what it means to be human." [25]

What if, in our social media engagement, we were to strive to help fulfill this mission? What if we were to look for opportunities to share "stuff that matters"?

It would require that we look for stories that inspire us, lift us up, and help us understand humanity at a deeper level. And then it would require that we share those meaningful stories with others.

Are you up for the challenge? SoulPancake is the perfect place to start.

Action: Look for opportunities to share "stuff that matters" on your social feeds, including the powerful content available through SoulPancake.

78

CULL RESPONSIBLY AND RESPECTFULLY

Since social media has grown so rapidly over the past few years, many of us have accumulated friends who we may not want to stay friends with. That's totally understandable. After all, that happens with friends that we have in our offline worlds, too.

However, when it comes to eliminating friends from your friend list, it's important to do so in a way that is respectful to others and to yourself.

If your reason for removing a friend from your connections is because that person is intimidating, bullying, or abusing you in some way, don't just remove that person as a friend. Save proof of their behavior, and if you are underage, please show this to a trusted adult. Then block that person, if possible, and report the behavior. Use whatever security measures you have available to you on that social platform in order to prevent that person from getting in contact with you again.

If your reason for removing a friend is that you no longer keep in touch with them or maybe don't even remember who they are or why you became friends with them, then likely the best thing to do is simply unfriend them or unfollow them. There's simply no need to remain connected, and this can be done easily without them being alerted to it.

If your reason is that you want to keep a certain channel for only your closest friends but still want to remain in contact, then reach out to the friends you want to remove. Explain why you're doing so and ask if they can be friends with you on a different channel instead.

Action: When you want to remove a friend on a specified social network, proceed with respect for yourself and others. Doing so, you'll be able to create groups of friends and connections on each channel that are right for you.

79

BE A DODO

Our furry (and feathered) friends have definitely made their marks on social media, and sometimes they can bring joy into our lives like nothing else. Whether we need a laugh or a cry or to be reminded that humanity is good, we can find the perfect animal story for the occasion. Sometimes even a funny cat meme does the trick.

The Dodo is one of my favorite brands on social media dedicated to sharing stories featuring our animal companions, and there are literally thousands of others. [26]

Just search for baby animals and you'll be laughing and crying happy tears in no time.

So much joy comes from furry friends, so when you get the chance, spread the joy…from The Dodo or somewhere else.

Action: When you see those heart-warming animal stories or the funny pet memes that make you laugh, share them with others. If you enjoyed them, your friends will too.

80

UNDERSTAND THE LACK OF TONE

Are you a jokester? That person who loves to make provocative comments at parties or ask questions just to get the debates started? Do you get a thrill out of playing devil's advocate?

That may be all well and good at in-person social events or around the dinner table. On social media, however, it's another story altogether. The posts you make on social are not private. They are out there for the world to see…and comment back.

Also, when you post on social media, all you are sharing is text. There's no way to communicate your inflection, your body language, the look in your eyes…all those things that convey your tone when you're speaking with people in person. They help others understand the underlying meaning of what it is that you're saying, and on social media those things are absent.

Tone means so much. Are you saying it light-heartedly? Is there humor in your eyes? Are you overwhelmed with sadness? None of these things can be perceived on social because it lacks that in-person element.

While your attempt at being funny or provocative with your friends in person may go over very well, that same comment made on social may achieve a completely different result. In fact, it may backfire on you entirely. Then you'll have to deal with damage control when it's too late to "undo" what's been done.

Action: Avoid posting comments that can be misconstrued through written text.

81

SHARE VIDEOS YOU LOVE

They make us laugh; they make us cry. Sometimes they resonate truth in a way that really hits home. Videos give us glimpses into the world and the hearts of people trying to change it.

By sharing a video that really strikes a chord with you, you're sharing a bit of yourself with the ones you love in the hopes that the video will have the same positive impact on them.

There are some videos out there that could melt the coldest hearts and inspire us all to be better, do better, try harder to help others. There are other videos that remind us so much of experiences we've had. They make us laugh and feel like the video so perfectly captures our experiences. There are others that simply bring joy because they are filled with pure delight.

And sometimes, they're just hilarious. Of course, everyone's humor is different, but there are those types of humor that just seem to resonate with everyone. A laugh that is absolutely contagious and that doesn't hurt anyone else is absolutely gold! That kind of laughter does so much good for everyone.

Some of my favorite places for inspiring and entertaining video resources on social are the following:

- The Dodo [26]
- The Holderness Family [27]
- NTD Inspired Life [28]

- LADbible [29]
- Oprah Winfrey Network [30]

Action: Share the videos that touch your heart and make you laugh. If they made a positive difference to you, they'll make a difference to others.

82

INVITE PEOPLE TO GROUPS

Adding people to groups without their permission occurs regularly on Facebook, and it's a huge no-no. Many of you have likely experienced this. A friend wants to share his or her new business or charity or fundraiser or whatever, so she or he creates a Facebook group for it and adds every friend on Facebook as a member. Why? Group members get notifications when others post in the group (although this can be turned off in settings), so there can be more exposure via groups than through profiles or pages.

Some friends will receive the addition to this new group with warmth, others with resentment. At that point, things become more complicated. Many friends won't want to leave the group for fear of hurting their friend's feelings. So instead, they get continuously more aggravated with the group postings because they don't know how to turn them off. Or they turn off the group notifications and never hear anything from the group, as if they are not members, which has defeated the original purpose.

If you have something new and exciting you want to share with your friends, there are better ways to do it.

1. If you have a new business, create a business page and invite your friends to like it.
2. If you want to create a group for your business to inspire more engagement and provide people a place to ask

questions, great. Invite friends to it rather than adding them without asking.
3. If you want to create a group for members to share more private deals or thoughts with each other (think of support groups, local advocacy groups, etc.), then create the group and, as above, invite people to join it. In this case, you'll want to target group members based on specific interests.

Following this simple practice will create a much more enjoyable experience for everyone.

Action: Invite people to join your group rather than adding them without asking.

83

JOIN THE CHEER SQUAD

Social media has made it possible for us to stay more aware of what our friends are going through and how they are feeling much of the time. So the next time one of your social media connections is down in the dumps, do something about it...and I don't mean just post a sympathy remark. That shows support, but does it actually help them cheer up? Maybe not. Do something that will.

Find the perfect video and send it in a private message. Search out the best e-card for the moment, and send it for private viewing. Or maybe you should just pick up the phone or pop on over to your friend's house. Now, isn't that a thought.

In our moments of sadness, we often crave human connection more than anything, even if we don't know it. A post and a text don't always give us what we need. Sometimes what we need is the sound of someone else's voice on the other end of the line. We need to hear that they care.

And sometimes we just need a hug. It always feels great to be the one giving it.

Action: When your friends need cheering up, do everything you can to help. If social media resources are all that's available, use those. If you can pick up the phone, do that. And if you can drop by for an in-person visit, that may be just what the doctor ordered.

84

FILTER YOUR FILTERS

Photographers and graphics designers have long since been applying various filters to enhance specific elements of their photos. When those filters became available to us "regular people," it was suddenly like we could all be our own amateur photographers, using borders and enhancing colors.

Unfortunately, filters and editing tools are also used by professionals to edit the reality out of photos: removing wrinkles, slimming thighs, lifting bums, plumping lips, and so on. The result is a generation of unrealistic ideals and people of all ages thinking their real selves aren't good enough to be captured in photos.

Apps are thriving on this, selling "beauty" through editing. Of course, beauty does not come through editing. Each of us is beautiful in our own unique way. Unfortunately, many of us are also falling prey to the temptations these photo filters offer: smooth some skin here, remove a few wrinkles, take away any so-called blemishes.

As more and more of us succumb to the temptation of using these filters to edit our real selves out of photos, we perpetuate the myth that beauty is only skin deep.

It's time to start embracing our own beauty and loving ourselves for who we are. That's the only way we can help our children love themselves, too. So, the next time you want to filter a photo of yourself, remember how beautiful you really are and let the whole world see you for you. #NoFilter

Action: Choose to share photos that show the real you. Be brave enough to stop using filters that hide who you are.

85

BRIDGE THE GENERATION GAP

Baby boomers are the fastest-growing group of social media users. While at first many can seem daunted by the processes of learning a new "technology skill," most soon discover that it's not technology at all. In fact, it is one of the easiest ways to stay connected with their loved ones.

The reality is that gone are the days of picking up the phone to call our grandparents. We don't send letters in the mail. It's easy to forget that while our lives are busy and we struggle for time to fit everything in, they are thinking of us so often and would love more than anything to hear from us.

Social media gives them that.

In the most basic sense, it allows them to follow our postings. They can see our photos and share in our experiences in real time—long before we would ever send them photos through the mail or call them to tell them about something important that happened today. They get to walk alongside us in our journeys by following our social feeds.

However, when we take it a step further, it means even more. Instead of simply trusting that they're seeing what we post, we can set it up so that our loved ones are notified when we post something. We can take an extra few minutes to tag them in a post or to send them a personal message with a photo we just shared online.

We can also create private groups on some networks where

we could interact in a more personal way, like a Facebook family group.

By no means am I suggesting that social media contact should replace phone calls and in-person visits. It's simply a way to stay more connected during those in-between times. By making the extra effort to let our loved ones know we're thinking about them even when we're not seeing them or talking, we're making a difference beyond that which we can understand ourselves…until we walk in their shoes.

Action: Encourage your loved ones to get online, show them how to use social media, and make a bit of extra effort to send them content you know they'll enjoy.

86

GET FACE TO FACE

Sometimes texting and posting on social just don't do the trick. They don't accomplish what we need.

Text doesn't hold the same vibration as spoken word. It can be misconstrued in some cases, and in others it can create a disconnect because it feels impersonal. This goes for our personal lives as well as for business and professional interactions.

Sometimes we need to experience the more personal engagement that face-to-face (even via a web tool) experiences can provide. Sometimes we really need to hear our friend's or colleague's voice. Sometimes we need to see a friendly face. Luckily for us, social media allows us that opportunity.

Many social networking tools provide the ability to have video conferences. Skype is a long-standing trusted option. Google Hangouts is available for every person with a Google account. Through Facebook you can also make video calls to your friends. Tools like Facebook Live allow you to speak to transmit live video, as well as see and respond to comments from viewers in real time.

While texting or posting text may be easy, easy isn't always right. Seeing someone can have a personal, powerful impact that words can't.

Action: When more than words is required or when you want to establish a more personal connection, use available social tools to communicate through video instead.

87

KNOW WHERE YOUR KIDS SPEND TIME

Social media isn't going anywhere. It is here to stay, albeit in a constantly changing way. The social platforms we use now may not be around when our children get old enough to use social media, or they may still exist but be of no interest to new generations.

However, as our children start using social media, it's important for us to understand not only the social platforms we use but the social platforms they are using, too. Those may be entirely different things.

To help protect and communicate with our children, we need to understand where they are spending their time. So, ask them. Then get on there and see what it's all about. Maybe it will be something that holds interests for you, and maybe not. However, you'll be one step closer to understanding why it consumes so much of your child's time and, thus, understand your child better, too.

Action: Find out where your kids are spending time on social media, and learn the facts about those networks so you can understand your children better and help them stay safe.

88

AVOID ANYTHING TOO PERSONAL

Not sharing content that is overly personal and might compromise someone's safety seems pretty basic, right? The unfortunate reality is that so many social media users (perhaps even you) don't recognize the potential repercussions of their actions. They also don't realize that the default on many social channels is to make all content public. These default settings, if left as they are, mean that anyone can find what you post. Anyone.

Stop and think about what that really means…for you, your colleagues, your boss, your employees, your family, your children.

It's shocking when I see some of the content that parents post about their children. A complete photo of a newly earned driver's license certainly demonstrates how proud that parent is. However, consider the additional information it conveys to everyone else.

While we don't like to consider the fact that there are those Internet users who prey on anyone they can find, that is a reality. We need to do everything we can to keep those we love safe. That begins with being aware that personal information is best kept offline.

Action: Avoid sharing overly personal content about yourself or anyone else that you know.

89

SEEK HELP

Asking for help is often the fastest way to get the support we need, both in our personal and professional situations.

We all have those days when we're at a stopping point. We don't know how to go forward. There's a problem that's stumping us. We're in a dark place we don't know how to climb out of on our own. We need to reach out but don't know where to go.

The irony of that situation is that we spend many, many of our waking hours engaging on these "social" platforms that we often neglect to draw on when we need help. We forget that we are literally surrounded by hundreds of friends. While they may not all be our closest kindred spirits, when we take the time to ask for help, we find many warm, welcoming hearts who will support us in any way that they can.

However, no one can read your mind. When you need help, you have to ask.

Action: When you need support from friends, don't forget that you have a network of support on social media that's there for you. Reach out to them, and ask for the help that you need.

90

STAY OPEN-MINDED

Social media presents us with every view under the sun. We are met with varying belief systems that encompass everything from sports to religion to politics with everything in between. There are those who use social networks for consistent sharing of specific agendas. They are unwavering in their mindset and unwilling to consider perspectives that are different from theirs. That is their choice.

However, if we allow the multitude of opinions and beliefs we witness from others to inform our own views of the world, we can begin to understand other people more. We can broaden our own minds and our own perspectives. We may never come to agree with many of the belief systems we encounter. We may, though, gain a deeper understanding of and respect for others.

There is no place where we can witness more belief systems shared in one place than on social media. By staying open and aware that behind each shared opinion there is a human soul much like ours, there becomes no need to defend one's own perspectives. Rather we can gain an appreciation for the fact that while diverse in our thoughts and beliefs, we are all one people.

There is only one human race, after all, and the more we understand each other, the more we can all thrive.

Action: Stay open-minded as you engage on social media and give yourself the gift of gaining a deeper appreciation and understanding of others.

Social media reaches beyond borders, beyond belief systems, beyond cultural walls. It brings people together from so many ways of life and literally is like a glue that somehow binds all of us—the entire human race—together.

91

GIVE HELP

One way you can help yourself is to ask for help when you need it. Another way to do good is to be the one to give help when it's needed and to make a commitment to be there when you are needed. Don't be a bystander. When a friend asks for help, reach out, step in and offer what you can.

Every post or tweet you see makes a statement. It's one that expresses the thoughts of the poster. Sometimes those thoughts are on the surface. Sometimes they're deep. In all cases, they reflect more than what is actually there, as words always do. There is meaning behind them.

Just as we likely do not stand by when someone we are next to in person asks for some business advice or a personal helping hand, such is the case when we encounter these situations online. It's up to each of us to take our role as "friend" to mean all that the word actually stands for in the first place.

If you aren't sure whether someone needs help, ask. Send them a message. Pick up the phone and give them a call. Do what you need to do to find out if there is something you can do to help. Then act on that knowledge. Don't be a bystander, even on social media.

Action: Consider the meaning behind your friends' words and reach out to give support whenever you can.

92

PROMOTE EVENTS

Using social in support of the events you are attending does a great service beyond what you may recognize. Your attendance shows support of the organization putting on the event. Whether it's a fundraiser, a parent event at your child's school, or a networking event for business, you can make use of your social presence in a positive way.

Simply sharing the fact that you are going can spread the word about an organization that you believe in. It can lead to others rallying around in support of a cause. It can spread the word about a business you want others to support. It's basically your endorsement for something you believe in.

From a business perspective, this is a powerful way to help support the local organizations you buy from and to encourage others to shop there as well. Share a link to the event in advance to increase attendance and sell tickets. Post a photo of yourself and your friends or colleagues at the event itself.

Take the opportunity to support what you believe in and realize that your words on social can go farther than they ever could in person.

Action: Make use of your social networks to share and promote events you want to support.

93

CELEBRATE YOUR OWN SUCCESS

When great things happen in our lives, we want to share it. So share it. Put smiles on the faces of those you love by allowing them to be part of your own personal celebrations.

Whether these are business success milestones, children's achievements, something you're personally proud of accomplishing yourself, or something else. Those you are connected with on your social channels want to cheer you on. They want to celebrate you. So let them.

Keep in mind that sharing your successes is just one piece of your social engagement. You also want to be cheering on others, supporting them in their growth, sharing inspiration, and using your social channels in many other ways addressed in this book. If it's all about celebrating you, then it quickly turns into a "braggedy-brag" situation…and none of your connections want to be part of that.

Action: Share your successes so your online friend community can celebrate with you.

94

RESPOND

It's funny how this simple thing has now become an act that is no longer fully expected in the personal or business world. We get voicemails. We don't return them. We get emails. We leave them for days and then often forget. We get calls from family and don't answer them.

This lack of response, while somewhat expected today, provides a great opportunity for those who actually do respond. Responding sets you apart. It gives you credibility. It establishes trust.

As a personal practice, responding to your friends tells them that your door is open and that you will be there when they need you. It shows them you care.

As a business practice, responding to your customers online demonstrates good customer service and tells your customers that they are important to you. It's shocking how many organizations leave audience complaints, compliments, and reviews without any response whatsoever.

In every regard, a response is good for you and good for those to whom you are responding. It's a win-win for everyone.

Action: When someone reaches out to you online, respond.

95

RECOMMEND FAVORITE PLACES

All of us have those favorite places we love to frequent. Someone calls for coffee; we suggest the same place each time. For a night out for dinner, we have our favorite go-to that always leaves our bellies and our hearts feeling full. We shop at our favorite grocery stores, buy from our favorite local markets, and have our favorite specialty shops for gifts and every other product or service we need.

We also have those special spots that don't cost anything to visit but pay us back in spades: favorite hiking trails, much-loved camping spots, best place for lawn seats at the free outdoor theater. We've shared many great memories in those favorite spots, so we keep returning to them.

Of course, this isn't to say that we always stick to what's familiar. Sometimes, we get creative. We think outside the box. We try something new.

And then we return to our old favorites because they never let us down.

But do we tell people about them? Sometimes yes, sometimes no. Using social media to do this is a powerful endorsement. It tells not only our local neighbors but everyone who may come in contact with those places just how special we think they are and why.

Social media users trust the recommendations of their friends, whether they come in person or on any social platform. Take advantage of that power and spread the word about the places you love. Tweet a picture of your treat at the local café. Post a photo of your family at your favorite camping spot. Leave a review for your favorite local store.

Your recommendations have a powerful impact. Make them wisely.

Action: Spread the word about your favorite places on social media...except for *maybe* your private camping spot. Maybe, *just maybe*, you should keep that one to yourself.

96

USE SHARE BUTTONS

Like something you see on social that your favorite organization has posted? Don't keep it to yourself. Would you keep it to yourself if you received as a gift the most delicious fudge you've ever tasted? Well, in that case, perhaps. Unlike fudge, however, a share has no end.

When you like it, your like notifies the organization that posted it that you like the content. When you share it, your share tells the world that you like that content.

Which has the greater impact?

So many people click the like button without clicking share, and while this is a great first step, it doesn't help increase visibility for the organization you support. To help the organization grow, share their content. It's one very powerful way to tell the world that this organization is amazing and that the world needs to take more notice.

So, when your favorite organization serves up the most delicious fudge you've ever tasted, it's time you started sharing it…at least online. Then everyone can go get their own.

Action: If you really like something and want to make sure other people like it too, click the share button to spread the word.

97

AVOID USING SHARE BUTTONS

While sharing the great content from your favorite organizations translates into more visibility and success for them, it can be a detriment when content is shared from personal sources.

Now, if a friend of yours has shared an inspiring video or a meme that made you laugh your tail off, that's one thing. In this case, share it—just share it from the original posting source rather than from your friend's profile. Each time you share something from a friend's profile directly you could be compromising his or her privacy.

Many of us use certain social channels in very private ways, and ideally our privacy settings should be set to match our intended use. When we share photos of our family or something that's personal, that content is being shared intentionally with the networks we have chosen to connect with. If other people share those personal bits of content, it can feel like an invasion of privacy.

So, while you may be excited when you see your grandson's photo or your friend's new baby, it isn't your place to share those personal moments unless you are asked to do so. Instead, like it, love it, and use every emoticon possible to express your joy. Then let the original posters be the ones who share their personal moments with the world, rather than you.

Action: Avoid sharing personal or private content from your social media friends.

98

TELL YOUR STORY

While this can be powerful when you engage personally on social media, this one goes out especially to all the entrepreneurs out there.

Storytelling is one of the most powerful and yet overlooked ways to engage your audience in a meaningful way on social media. It is a tool that will set you apart because here's the truth: no one else (no other person, no other business, no other entrepreneur) has your story.

What makes storytelling such a powerful way to use social media for good?

- Stories establish connections.
- They create human experiences.
- They paint pictures and build emotional connections between people around the globe.

Stories are many things that your tribe craves from you. Stories are engaging, memorable, relatable, and personal. Stories preserve who we are.

There's no other tool or technique that can capture the core essence of an entrepreneur or business so completely as storytelling because, like nothing else, it sets you completely apart and shares the uniqueness that makes you you.

However, most entrepreneurs do not tell their own stories.

They get so caught up in creating and delivering their products and services, providing customer service, and promoting what they have to offer that they often forget to communicate with their tribe in a way that truly resonates and builds relationships.

Stop holding back. No one else has your story, so now's the time to start telling it, creating connections as you go.

Action: Make now the time when you start using social media to tell your story.

It is the end goals, the visions, the ultimate impact on the world that our collective stories make...those become legend, and legend lives forever.

99

RAISE YOUR VOICE

Our lives begin to end the day we become silent about things that matter. —Dr. Martin Luther King Jr.

Likely by now you've picked up on a common theme: your words are powerful. They matter. And social media magnifies them.

Engaging proactively on social media is like raising your voice to a global gramophone that broadcasts what you have to say to the world. By raising your voice, you impact lives far and wide. So, do it.

Raise your voice in celebration of life and all that is good. Raise your voice in support of those you love. Raise your voice as an advocate for all that you believe in. Raise your voice for those who cannot use their voice for themselves. Raise your voice to educate, to inspire, to spread joy, to uplift.

And always remember how very powerful your voice is. Remember and choose to raise your voice as one of the choir of many who are committed to using their social voices for good.

Action: Raise your voice on social media to do good.

100

OBSERVE MOMENTS OF SILENCE

Just as raising your voice can transcend boundaries of time and space to impact lives around the globe, so can your silence.

Sometimes posting nothing is the only way to do good.

Using social media for good requires a balance of posting and not posting, of liking and not liking, of commenting and not commenting, of sharing and not sharing, of raising your voice and being silent.

We need only recognize the right time for each action.

That knowledge lies within each of us. We have only to seek our own truth and do what we know to be right.

Don't be afraid of silence. It speaks volumes and is often just what the world needs.

Action: When you have no positive words to offer on social media, be strong and committed to yourself enough to be silent.

101

BE SOULCIAL

Using social media for good extends far beyond our individual selves, families and businesses. It requires a shift in the way we communicate from social media to **soul**cial media, which has a far-reaching impact on the world.

To put it simply, *soul*cial media is an elevated form of social media, through which users communicate authentically and ethically to create positive impacts.

With *soul*cial media communication comes responsibility—a responsibility to use your social media channels as a force for good.

Social media reaches beyond borders, beyond belief systems, beyond cultural walls. It brings people together from so many ways of life and literally is like a glue that somehow binds all of us— the entire human race—together. Social media is a force of the people and for the people. As such, it is of the planet and for the planet, too.

It is our responsibility to ensure we do our part to achieve an impact with our social media communication that will truly serve as a force for good…for the planet and its people.

The ways in which you can do this are simple, and many of them have been identified in this book. It isn't about grandiose ideas. It's about thinking through every post before you post it and considering the fact that all of your words generate impact. It's up to you to determine what kind of impact you want your words to have.

Some things to consider as you use social media for good:

- Every post generates an outcome, so choose your words wisely.
- Be authentic in your communication so people can see who you are at the core. It's who you are at the core that makes the difference.
- Social media is power. Know that. Understand that. Then proactively decide how you will use that power for good.
- Engage with other *soul*cial individuals. Working together and supporting each other will result in more positive change.
- Look for the changemakers, and share their stories.
- Consider how your words will make a positive difference for future generations.
- Remember that it only takes one negative post to make your social media audience forget all the good you stand for.
- Generating real impact happens without thought. However, in order to shape the impact you generate, you must do a lot of thinking in advance.
- The best way to affect positive change through your social media communication is to become the change you seek and portray that online as well as everywhere else.

So, in a nutshell, your mission, if you choose to accept it, is to change the world…one social media post at a time.

Action: Be *Soul*cial

Your mission, if you choose to accept it, is to change the world…one social media post at a time.

Resources That Support Using Social Media for Good

None of these lists are meant to be all-inclusive or complete. They only scratch the surface of all that is available to us online. I look forward to adding to these lists as time goes on, so please send me your favorites, too.

Inspiring TED and TEDx Talks

I asked my network online to share their favorite TED Talks. This list is a compilation of my favorites and theirs, in no particular order.

- "Every Kid Needs a Champion"—Rita Pierson
- "My Year of Saying Yes to Everything"—Shonda Rhimes
- "How Do You Define Yourself"—Lizzie Valesquez
- "I Got 99 Problems…Palsy Is Just One"—Maysoon Zayid
- "The Power of Vulnerability"—Brené Brown
- "Why the Only Future Worth Building Includes Everyone"—His Holiness Pope Francis
- "How to Find a Wonderful Idea"—OK Go
- "Why We Need to Imagine Different Futures"—Anab Jain
- "Know Your Worth, and Then Ask for It"—Casey Brown
- "Watch Me Play…the Audience"—Bobby McFerrin
- "Taking Imagination Seriously"—Janet Echelman
- "Stroke of Insight"—Jill Bolte Taylor
- "The Happy Secret to Better Work"—Shawn Achor
- "Your Elusive Creative Genius"—Elizabeth Gilbert
- "Pop an Ollie and Innovate!"—Rodney Mullen
- "The Surprising Habits of Original Thinkers"—Adam Grant

- "Grit: The Power of Passion and Perseverance"—Angela Lee Duckworth
- "The Power of Meaning You Can Improve"—Carol Dweck
- "The Danger of the Single Story"—Chimamanda Ngozi Adichie
- "The Power of Introverts"—Susan Cain
- "Embracing Otherness, Embracing Myself"—Thandie Newton
- "Educating a Neurodiverse World"—Brian Kinghorn
- "Trust, Morality—and Oxytocin"—Paul Zak
- "How to Rewire Your Brain"—Dr. Joe Dispenza
- "Building a Caring Economy"—Riane Eisler
- "My Philosophy for a Happy Life"—Sam Berns
- "How to Be Happy Every Day: It Will Change the World"—Jacqueline Way
- "Happiness Is All in Your Mind"—Gen Kelsang Nyema
- "The Art of Being Yourself"—Caroline McHugh
- "Got a Meeting? Take a Walk"—Nilofer Merchant

Crowdfunding, Giving, and Petition Platforms

When you're looking for ways to support nonprofit organizations, start-ups, education, or others in need or to lend your support by signing petitions, in addition to the few I highlighted previously, here are a few places you can go to search for opportunities. [31]

- Kiva
- Change.org
- Kickstarter
- Causecast
- iPetitions

- GoFundMe
- IndieGoGo
- Omaze
- CrowdRise
- JustGiving
- DonorsChoose
- Piggybackr

Organizations with Social Feeds That Do Good

Need to up your daily dose of joy? Visit one of these pages online. There are thousands and thousands of organizations out there committed to doing good in the world with the social content they publish, and I've touched on only a few here in this book. What follows (in no particular order) is a very small segment that includes some of my favorites and favorites submitted by friends online.

- The Universe—Mike Dooley
- Amy McNaughton
- Power of Positivity
- Upworthy
- Dalai Lama
- The Dodo
- Deepak Chopra
- Awesome Pics
- OWN TV and Oprah Winfrey
- NTD Inspired Life
- National Geographic
- Inspirational Quotes Hub
- Ellen DeGeneres
- Daily Animal Cuteness
- The Secret

- LADbible
- Animalkind Stories
- Humankind Stories
- The Holderness Family
- Tiny Buddha
- We Love Animals
- Delish
- Power of the Law of Attraction
- Animal Rescue Home
- Anita Moorjani
- SoulPancake
- Ami Vitale
- Tasty
- Scott Stabile
- Elephant Journal
- Special Books by Special Kids
- Raise the Vibe

And don't forget to follow me. I promise to share uplifting content on all of my social channels. Here's where to find me:

- Facebook: @franceslearycoach
- Instagram: @franceslearycoach
- Twitter: @francesleary
- LinkedIn: @francesleary

I look forward to soulcializing with you. Let's make the world a better place together.

REFERENCES

(1) Dooley, Mike, and Hope Koppelman. *Love Your Life in 30 Days: The Essential Companion to the OnlineVideo Course.* Orlando: TUT Enterprises, Inc., 2016.

(2) *Birthday Wishes for Your Facebook Friends.* Birthday Wishes Expert. 9 Set 2017. <https://www.birthdaywishes.expert/happy-birthday-wishes-for-facebook-friends/>.

(3) *Top 100+ Original and Funny Happy Birthday Memes.* Birthday Wishes Expert. 9 Set 2017. <https://www.birthdaywishes.expert/top-100-original-and-funny-happy-birthday-memes/>.

(4) About. Change.org, Inc. 24 Oct. 2017. <https://www.change.org/about>

(5) About Us. Upworthy. 29 Oct. 2017. <http://www.upworthy.com/about>.

(6) Kid-Activities. *Pinterest.* 11 Nov. 2017. <https://www.pinterest.com/explore/kid-activities/>.

(7) Easy Activities for Kids. *Facebook.* 11 Nov. 2017. <https://www.facebook.com/EasyActivitiesForKids/>.

(8) Fun Family Crafts. *Facebook.* 11 Nov. 2017. <https://www.facebook.com/FunFamilyCrafts/>.

(9) Make and Takes. *Facebook.* 11 Nov. 2017. <https://www.facebook.com/makeandtakes/>.

(10) Quirky Momma. *Facebook.* 11 Nov. 2017. <https://www.facebook.com/QuirkyMomma/>.

(11) National.Earth. *Instagram.* 11 Nov. 2017. < https://www.instagram.com/national.earth/>.

(12) Inspirational Quotes. *Facebook.* 11 Nov. 2017. <https://www.facebook.com/InspirationalQuotesHub/>.

(13) Inspirationalqu0tes. *Instagram.* 11 Nov. 2017. <https://www.instagram.com/inspirationalqu0tes/>.

(14) Home. *Stencil.* 11 Nov. 2017. <https://getstencil.com/>.

(15) Home. *PicMonkey.* 11 Nov. 2017. <https://www.picmonkey.com/>.

(16) Home. *Canva.* 11 Nov. 2017. <https://www.canva.com/>.

(17) Home. Pixabay. 23 Oct. 2017. <https://pixabay.com/>.

(18) Home. Pexels. 23 Oct. 2017. <https://www.pexels.com/>.

(19) About. *Kiva.* 27 Sept. 2017. <https://www.kiva.org/about>.

(20) Home. Kickstarter. 16 Oct. 2017. <https://www.kickstarter.com/>.

(21) *At Home By Myself…With You.* Dir. Kris Booth. Pocket Change Films, 2010. iTunes: <https://itunes.apple.com/ca/movie/at-home-by-myself-with-you/id364612915>.

(22) Tasty. *Facebook.* 14 Sept. 2017. <https://www.facebook.com/buzzfeedtasty/>.

(23) Delish. *Facebook.* 14 Sept. 2017. <https://www.facebook.com/delish/>.

(24) Simple Balance: Real Food Nutrition. *Facebook.* 14 Sept. 2017. <https://www.facebook.com/SimpleBalance/>.

(25) SoulPancake. *Facebook.* 15 Sept. 2017. <https://www.facebook.com/soulpancake/>.

(26) The Dodo. *Facebook.* 18 Sept. 2017. <https://www.facebook.com/thedodosite/>.

(27) The Holderness Family. *Facebook.* 22 Oct. 2017. <https://www.facebook.com/TheHoldernessfamily/>.

(28) NTD Inspired Life. *Facebook.* 22 Oct. 2017. <https://www.facebook.com/TheHoldernessfamily/>.

(29) LADBible. *Facebook.* 22 Oct. 2017. <https://www.facebook.com/LADbible/>.

(30) OWN: Oprah Winfrey Network. *Facebook.* 22 Oct. 2017. <https://www.facebook.com/ownTV/>.

(31) *21 Top Crowdfunding Sites: Categories and Comparision [2018 Update].* YouCaring. 5 Feb. 2018. <https://www.youcaring.com/blog/2016/top-crowdfunding-sites>.

(32) *The Definitive Fact-Checking Site and Reference Source for Urban Legends, Folklore, Myths, Rumors and Misinformation.* Snopes. 8 Nov. 2018. <https://www.snopes.com/>.

(33) Today's News, Entertainment, Video, Ecards and More and Someecards. Someecards. 22 Oct. 2017. <https://www.someecards.com/>.

CPSIA information can be obtained
at www.ICGtesting.com
Printed in the USA
BVHW07s2045110918
527206BV00001B/10/P